Improving Professional Learning through In-House Inquiry

Also available from Bloomsbury

Forthcoming

Improving Professional Learning through In-House Inquiry

DAVID MIDDLEWOOD
AND IAN ABBOTT

Bloomsbury Academic
An imprint of Bloomsbury Publishing Plc

B L O O M S B U R Y
LONDON · NEW DELHI · NEW YORK · SYDNEY

Bloomsbury Academic
An imprint of Bloomsbury Publishing Plc

50 Bedford Square	1385 Broadway
London	New York
WC1B 3DP	NY 10018
UK	USA

www.bloomsbury.com

BLOOMSBURY and the Diana logo are trademarks of Bloomsbury Publishing Plc

First published 2015

British Library Cataloguing-in-Publication Data
A catalogue record for this book is available from the British Library.

ISBN: HB:	978-1-4725-7083-3
PB:	978-1-4725-7082-6
ePDF:	978-1-4725-7084-0
ePub:	978-1-4725-7085-7

Library of Congress Cataloging-in-Publication Data
A catalog record for this book is available from the Library of Congress.

Typeset by Newgen Knowledge Works (P) Ltd., Chennai, India
Printed and bound in India

CONTENTS

ABOUT THE AUTHORS

David Middlewood is currently a research fellow at Warwick University's Centre for Education Studies. He previously worked at the Universities of Leicester and Lincoln, following a successful career in schools, which included ten years as a headteacher. David has published eighteen books on educational topics, many on people-leadership and management, as well as on practitioner research. He has researched widely in the United Kingdom and in other countries such as South Africa and New Zealand, where he has been a visiting professor, as well as in Greece and Seychelles. Some of his research areas include school collaboration, appraisal, support staff, diversity, team performance and leadership succession planning. He was co-editor of two practitioner journals for several years. He has been a researcher in residence for a group of schools and led conferences and seminars on both staff and student research.

Ian Abbott is associate professor and director of the Centre for Education Studies at the University of Warwick. He successfully led the reorganization of the Institute of Education and the establishment of the Centre for Education Studies at the University of Warwick. Prior to higher education he worked in schools and colleges in senior leadership roles for a number of years. He has worked in partnership with a number of external organizations, including Teach First and Teaching Leaders to develop bespoke Masters level qualifications. He has collaborated with a number of schools and colleges on a variety of research projects. His research interests include education policy, school collaboration, the Pupil Premium and initial teacher education. He has published widely on education policy, teacher education and school and college leadership.

David and Ian have taught and tutored together on various Masters programmes, both in the United Kingdom and in Africa and Greece. They have also led the Masters programme for 'Teaching Leaders' and wrote the standard text on leadership dissertations, 'Achieving Success in Your Leadership Project', in 2013.

FIGURES

CONTRIBUTORS

Cathy Francis-Wright is a professional development coordinator in a large further education college in the English Midlands; this involves leading development initiatives in working with other colleges across the region.

Ayman Hefnawi is a Maths teacher at Abu Dhabi Education Council. He is currently the head of Mathematics in a public school.

Richard Parker was the principal of a large 14–19 secondary school and community college (his second headship) for nine years. He is now a consultant and has worked part-time for the Universities of Northampton and Warwick, United Kingdom.

Auruna Rajah is a former advisor in the Abu Dhabi Council Public Private Partnership (PPP). She currently works for the Abu Dhabi Education Council as a Maths education adviser.

Sue Robinson was headteacher of a large primary school in England's second largest city, leading it to being a nationally recognized high achieving school. She worked as a key figure at the National College until 2014. She is currently an active director of a large educational foundation and works also for the University of Warwick, UK, where she received her doctorate in 2010.

Derek Warren is standards and performance manager in a large further education college in the English Midlands; he has previously been director of general education and of 14–19 partnerships as well as an associate inspector.

Philip Whitehead is a senior teaching fellow in the Centre for Education Studies at the University of Warwick, UK. Among various responsibilities, he acted as tutor and supervisor of the university's MA study group in Abu Dhabi.

Uwem Umana has been an advisor in the Abu Dhabi Education Public Private Partnership (PPP) project for five years. He currently works for Abu Dhabi Vocational training Institute (ADVETI) as a teacher of English in their military project.

PREFACE

With both of us having been heavily involved in professional development of one kind or another over many years, first as teachers and leaders in schools, and later in universities, we have had a constant interest in the topic of how people in education can continue to improve. From early days of picking a course from a list, almost at will, to the modern recognition that only teachers and lecturers who are fully professional learners can be effective, the understanding of what benefits the pupils and students most has grown massively.

In more recent times, as tutors of postgraduate students, virtually all of them teachers, we found the process of practitioner research a fascinating one, which teachers excitedly told us had, in many cases, revolutionized their practice and their thinking about that practice. What was particularly noticeable was that it did not seem to matter whether the teacher was a newly qualified teacher (NQT) or one who had been teaching for twenty to thirty years – the enthusiasm was the same. We found this excitement replicated in various countries where we had the opportunity to teach and tutor, both in developed and in developing nations. As the idea of pupil or student 'voice' began to take root in various forward-looking schools, the idea of extending this in-house inquiry to include the actual learners in the process was a natural progression, and we both became heavily involved, both in schools themselves and in school student conferences organized on university sites. This student voice concept, as noted in Chapter Three, is in fact well established in, for example, the Scandinavian countries and in the Republic of South Africa the structures for its use were put in place at the founding of a new education system in 1994, although not fully utilized to date.

The impact of much of this practitioner inquiry was in the field of the teachers' and lecturers' own professional development and their personal and professional learning in general. Some schools and colleges found their provision of learning opportunities for staff of all kinds completely changed by practitioner inquiry, both by staff and by students, carried out in their own working contexts. After all, where a staff member has identified a specific aspect of his or her practice that could be improved, it is obvious that they would need help in developing that aspect – through some form of professional learning. While we recognize that there are of course other ways than in-house inquiry to identify developmental needs, we believe that this practitioner research offers one of the most compelling and accessible means of doing so. Furthermore, the process itself of carrying out the inquiry has significant benefits in a wider sense and, as some examples in the book show, changes the whole ethos of an institution – to the advantage of everyone there.

All these were the stimulus for the writing of this book, using the experiences of so many of the staff and students as described above. As we carried out the research for this book, interviewing numerous people, including those whose experiences are recorded as case examples, we need hardly add that, as professionals ourselves, we inevitably learned a great deal. This is we hope reflected in the writing of this book.

The structure of the book is straightforward. The first three chapters address the two key elements of the book's premise. Chapter One introduces the context of modern professional learning and outlines issues of effectiveness, while Chapter Two describes what is involved in developing a school or college committed to becoming 'research-engaged'. Chapter Three concentrated on the ultimately most important people – the actual pupils and students – and how they can be closely involved in school or college improvement through in-housed inquiry. Chapters Four and Six each focus on an aspect of professional learning via inquiry-the individual in the classroom approach and the whole organizational aspect. Research can be seen as a 'co-operative social practice' (Rogers, 2014), and Chapter Five is concerned with this collaborative approach, often through teams in schools or colleges.

If, as Gunter, Hall and Mills (2014: 166) suggest, 'the best teachers teach through stories and storytelling,' then our illustrations of what individuals actually did (mostly in their own words), add hugely to the book's value. While we give many such case examples throughout these chapters to illustrate how people have enacted what we describe, Chapters Seven, Eight, Nine and Ten each offer a detailed case study of how different kinds of institutions have successfully developed their cultures and practices with professional learning at the heart to dramatically improve the outcomes for all in the place.

Richard Parker describes how a large secondary school placed in-house inquiry at the centre of its development, with a huge impact on student and staff culture. In Chapter Eight, Sue Robinson describes how an under-performing urban primary school was transformed by a focus on staff learning. Institutions in the post-compulsory sector are usually large colleges and in Chapter Nine Derek Warren and Cathy Francis-Wright tell how, through a rigorous emphasis on identifying developing needs of staff roles, individuals and teams in their Further Education College grew significantly in confidence and ability, leading to greatly improved teaching and learning. In countries with very centralized educational systems, 'CPD' or 'training' is usually dictated nationally for any new initiatives at government level, with little or no scope for individual schools to adjust according to local context. The case study schools in Chapter Ten therefore are particularly interesting in showing how individual 'trainers' were able to develop local teacher CPD through their own research inquiries.

Finally, in Chapter Eleven, we try briefly to draw together some of the above issues and take a tentative look ahead in this field. This book is concerned with enabling in-house inquiry or research to become embedded in the school's or college's practice and, as in our Chapter Seven, and in, for example, Gunter, Hall and Mills's book (2014) on policy research, this embedding is so crucial for success.

We would like to thank various people for their support in writing this book, especially Trish Caswell for her invaluable work on the manuscript, Brian Everest for his ideas on and examples of professional learning in a special school context, and of course the other authors, all highly successful practitioners, who have contributed the case study chapters. All the teachers and students we have worked with over many years have inevitably been the inspiration for most of the ideas given here and we thank them for all their commitment and professionalism. We thank those at Bloomsbury, especially Alison and Kasia, for their encouragement. David wishes to dedicate his work to a true professional colleague, Tony Pulford, who sadly died during the book's production. Finally, David thanks Jacqui and Ian thanks Deb for all their personal support during the writing of this book.

David Middlewood and Ian Abbott
March 2015

ABBREVIATIONS

ADEC	Abu Dhabi Education Council
ADVETI	Abu Dhabi Vocational Training Institute
BECTA	British Educational Communications and Technology Agency
CPD	Continuous Professional Development
DfE	Department for Education
EQ	Emotional Quotient
FE	Further Education (i.e. post-compulsory education)
FSM	Free School Meals
GCSE	General Certificate in Secondary Education
HE	Higher Education
HMI	Her Majesty's Inspector
HNC	Higher National Certificate
HND	Higher National Diploma
HoD	Head of Department
ICT	Information Communications Technology
IIP	Investors in People
ITE	Initial Teacher Education
LT	Licensed Teacher
M Level	Masters Degree
NFER	National Foundation for Educational Research
NPQH	National Professional Qualification in Headship
NQT	Newly Qualified Teacher
NVQ	National Vocational Qualification
OECD	Organization for Economic and Cultural Development
OFSTED	Office for Standards in Education
PHSE	Personal, Health and Social Education
PLC	Professional Learning Community
PPP	Public Private Partnership
QPL	Quality Performance Leader
SIP	School Improvement Partner
SIP	School Improvement Plan
SSAT	Specialist Schools and Academies Trust
TA	Teaching Assistant
VAK	Verbal, Aural, Kinaesthetic
VLE	Virtual Learning Environment

PART ONE
Principles

CHAPTER ONE

Effectiveness in professional learning and CPD

Introduction

Continuous professional development (CPD) and professional learning for staff has been identified as one of the key factors in school improvement, both in developed countries (Bolam et al., 2000) and in developing countries (Dalin and Rust, 1996). Recent developments in several countries, including England, have signalled major changes in the way in which educational organizations manage the provision of professional learning and CPD as well as the initial training of teachers. In particular, there is a move towards greater ownership by individual institutions of the management of their learning needs and provision. These developments are a reflection of a system-wide move towards greater organizational autonomy which is taking place in many countries across the world, including some of the burgeoning economies such as China and India. This chapter deals with the key purposes of professional learning and CPD and why it is a crucial factor in bringing about educational improvement in schools and colleges. In this chapter, the following are considered:

- The definitions, purposes and importance of professional learning and CPD,
- developing a culture of effective professional learning,
- different forms of professional learning,
- issues concerning effectiveness of professional learning,
- identifying and meeting the needs of staff and students and
- impact and evaluation of professional learning and CPD, including cost-effectiveness.

The definitions, purposes and importance of professional learning and CPD

Historically CPD is the generic term that has been used to describe the professional development of staff in schools and colleges. More recently the term 'professional learning' has started to replace CPD. Increasingly CPD has been associated with specific courses or programmes while professional learning is a much broader concept involving a range of development opportunities. For the purposes of this book, we will use both terms. We use CPD to mean more formal, organized training/learning, and we use professional learning in a much broader sense, incorporating all kinds of development, which may include formal CPD.

Some form of professional development is central to the career progression of practitioners in a wide range of professional occupations. For example, in a book on career progression and development in the accountancy profession, Lindsay (2015) notes that CPD is still widely used there but that the term is becoming a little 'passé' (ibid.: 15) and she links it more significantly with 'life-long learning'. It should not be confused with the related concepts of 'on-the-job learning' or 'in-service training', which are more limited. Professional learning and CPD are both wider concepts and can involve a broader range of teaching and learning styles and approaches in a variety of settings inside and outside the workplace. The development of professionals is related both to the professional identity of individual staff and to the objectives of the organization they are employed by (Galloway, 2000). It is the marrying of these two, the individual and the organization, that lies at the core of effectiveness of professional development. This is a topic we discuss later in the chapter and return to in later chapters where we propose ways of achieving and evaluating this effectiveness.

The three words of the phrase 'continuing professional development' are interesting in themselves. Obviously, 'continuing' suggests that it is something that will be ongoing throughout a person's professional career. The word 'professional' itself carries various connotations and the notion of professionalism has been debated and indeed contested, including the question as to whether teaching is a profession in the same sense that medicine and law are clearly accepted as such. As well as its practitioners being qualified and initially trained, professionals may at the least be seen as having:

- a degree of autonomy,
- an acceptance of accountability, and
- acceptance of an ethical code of conduct or practice.

'Development' should be distinguished from 'training'. Learning via training has the connotation of 'highly specific, content-driven and targeted programmes geared to knowledge acquisition and information-giving' (Law and Glover, 2000: 247). It has a place in any professional's career as new skills and information are often needed in order for a person to be up to date in their field of expertise – we are not likely to trust a lawyer who does not know that a law has been changed or a doctor who uses obsolete equipment! The word 'development' however implies concern for the practitioners as people in their learning, either professional or personal, or both. It is therefore closely linked with personal development, because the attitudes, feelings and motivation of the persons concerned are necessary if they are to improve. Professional learning further develops this theme because it implies a deeper and wider form of development than that often associated with CPD, which is often linked with skills acquisition.

Educational organizations should theoretically be ideally placed for this professional development because their core purpose is to enable learning through effective teaching. Whatever form they take, from pre-school to education for the Third Age, they have the quality of education and learning at the core of what they do. Since all staff in an educational organization have learning and the enabling of learning as their key purpose, all activities within the organization should have an ultimate focus on learning. Staff who are employed to carry out maintenance, clean, provide meals and transport are all involved because they are trying to ensure that student learning takes place effectively in the best possible environment and in the best possible condition. Office staff who are involved in dealing with administrative tasks also undertake these tasks ultimately to facilitate effective learning. Teaching and lecturing staff have learning as their prime focus, and therefore it is essential that each member of staff has the opportunity to develop themselves within their own roles and become continuous learners. Professional development therefore needs to be at the heart of every educational institution, as it strives to improve teaching and learning. In her work on school improvement, Harris (2002) has reported that improving schools have frequent interchange and professional dialogue, that is, about teaching and learning, at a formal and informal level throughout the institution.

A good deal of educational research and literature supports the view that the most effective teachers are those who themselves are good learners and continue to learn, (see, e.g. Blandford, 2000; Stoll et al., 2003; Early and Bubb, 2004, Middlewood et al., 2005; and Brooks, 2012). Therefore, a school or college which is able to encourage all its employees to embrace a commitment to their own learning and development should be the one that is most effective in pupil or student learning. Day (1999) has also claimed that teachers' professional development is an essential component of successful change in schools and colleges. Additionally, Muijs et al. (2004) have argued that effective professional development has a positive impact on curriculum development, and Bush and Middlewood (2013) note that the provision of effective professional development can be a significant factor in both recruitment and retention in organizations. We can therefore identify several ways in which effective professional learning and CPD is vital to the ongoing success of any educational organization.

If we pause here to consider what we mean overall by 'professional learning' and its significance, we can perhaps more readily deal with the management issues relating to it.

If a teacher or lecturer as a member of the education profession is to be effective, s/he will normally have decided to train to be such and acquired certain skills and capabilities to enhance certain personal qualities inherent in them as a person. Clearly, such skills will need to be refreshed and updated as time passes and/or in the light of new policy requirements. Also, cliché though this is, the world of education and indeed the world itself will be significantly different from when a person began in the profession. Thus, if we compare a teacher of twenty years' experience with that person after, say, four years, the teacher will be different and so will be the person! In this century, such a person has to be used to change as a constant, and the aware, intelligent person will be learning how to manage that change in a positive way. S/he will sometimes complain about a specific change or changes (as humans, we all do!), but the true professional will adapt and thrive. THIS is learning! As has been noted many times, change equals learning! In the modern world, acquiring knowledge is relatively easy. One's children and grandchildren usually 'know' as much or more about the latest technology, for example! But knowledge does not equal learning – as Eric Hoffer pointed out: 'In times of change, the learners will inherit the earth, whereas the knowers will be beautifully equipped for a world that no longer exists!'

For us therefore, a professional learner is one who is continually adapting to new contexts and situations and in doing so enables their pupils and students to do the same. The task of effective organizations is to offer opportunities for them to be able to do this. If change equals learning, then learning equals change and we like the story of the headteacher faced with a teacher who proudly claimed that he did not need any CPD because he had been teaching for twenty years and why should he change? The reply was:

> I think you mean you have been teaching one year; you have just done it twenty times!

Developing a culture of effective professional learning and CPD

The term 'learning organization' is often used to describe an organization that has a positive approach to professional learning. This is an all-encompassing phrase that has its origins in the business community and is widely associated with a dynamic and successful organization. Revans

(1982) originally proposed the equation that the rate of learning in an organization must be equal to, or greater than, the rate of change. A consistent feature of education in many countries has been the increasing pace of change as the government has striven to raise standards by a deluge of education policy (Abbott et al., 2013). Schools and colleges have been – and still are – under constant pressure to change and thus the need for organizations to be continuously learning and developing as they strive to foster and maintain success, is greater than ever. Such schools and colleges have to:

- Focus their energies and activities on learning, recognizing that learning may come in many different forms as appropriate to a wide range of learners.

- Establish and develop an ethos and ethic of enquiry.

- Recognize that learning can come from many sources – not just from formal teaching; external networks and stakeholders such as parents also contribute to learning.

- Accept that learning is a lifelong process and that the organization's role is in making a contribution to this process.

- Be in a continuous transformational state.

Working in a school or college that has these characteristics is likely to be not only interesting and challenging, but also ultimately rewarding! In order to 'be better', the organization will continually challenge the status quo and they (the staff and leaders) will strive to find 'new and better ways of doing business' (Holyoke et al., 2012: 437). Developing a learning organization will require a common sense of purpose which will be allied to a drive for continuous improvement. McCharen et al. (2011: 689), when researching innovation in schools, reported that a 'sense of shared purpose is a notable aspect of a learning organisation' and that this sharing was rooted in 'shared commitments to values, such as the integrity of teaching or the need for social justice'. Abbott and Bush (2013: 598) claim that in outstanding primary schools 'there was a strong emphasis on mentoring and coaching' and 'individual professional development was strongly supported' with an emphasis on 'a clear vision, accepted by all the participants, around improving the life chances of the children who attend the school'. A shared purpose will drive a school or college forward and will enable it to constantly innovate and change because it is able to make best use of its people through their own learning. This learning can take a number of forms and a learning school or college should:

- promote learning as a means to an end,
- develop learning as a process,

- facilitate learning how to learn,

- ensure learning provides knowledge which is worth pursuing for its own sake.

Learning as a means to an end refers to learning that is considered by the learner as being worthwhile and leads to tangible outcomes. In many societies, especially developing countries, education is seen as a means of securing economic success, improving life chances and securing a better future. This is often associated with specific skill acquisition and a formal qualification.

Accepting that learning is a process and the development of the skills of learning enables the learner to take their learning and apply it to a variety of contexts (Middlewood et al., 2005). Developing a passion for the subject area they teach is an essential part of a teacher's role in a learning school or college. This helps staff in their valuing learning for its own sake. At different stages of their career, staff in schools and colleges may be required to undertake specific learning to gain a qualification to enable them to obtain promotion or to be able to continue to practice. An example of this type of learning is the requirement in many countries for aspiring headteachers and principals to have formal leadership qualifications. Many undertake this form of qualification to enable them to be able to apply for senior posts rather than learning, because they value the pursuit of knowledge.

Developing a culture of continuous learning and development requires the organization to value staff and to encourage professional development rather than simply providing a range of training courses. As noted above, development values staff as people in their learning, either professional or personal, or both. The employee will ideally have a degree of ownership

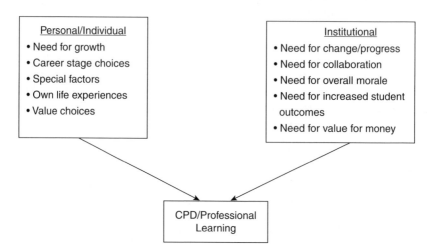

FIGURE 1.1 *In-house influences in CPD/professional learning.*

about the kind of support, training and development they require to improve performance. A number of commentators on teacher development such as Day (1999) and Ribbins (2008) argue that development relates to individual history as well as the current situation and that the work educational staff do 'is bound up with their lives, their histories, the kind of person they have been and have become' (Day, 1999: 124). Figure 1.1 illustrates the main in-house influences on the development of professional learning and CPD.

Significant learning and an appropriate culture for effective professional learning and CPD occurs when staff are committed to a fundamental approach to learning, rather than a 'surface or quick-fix short-term training approach' (Piggot-Irvine, 2010: 242). By ensuring proper opportunities for professional learning, a school or college will be able to maximize the potential for effective change and development.

Different forms of professional learning and CPD

The actual provision of CPD and the opportunities for professional learning may take several different forms and the specific form(s) often may need to take account of the specific context, of the school or college, the team or the individual. Each school or college has its own specific context; both in time and place, and all professional development will have a different emphasis depending on a range of circumstances. There will be significant differences, for example, between countries where the focus in a developing country might be to ensure adequate school attendance for all young people, compared to a country where the emphasis is placed on achieving improved test scores for 18-year-old school/college leavers. Internally there will also be differences among rural, suburban and inner city schools, which will be reflected in the workforce in the institution. Indeed the composition of the workforce may be another factor influencing the type of professional development available with young, highly mobile members of staff often having different needs to those of their more experienced and perhaps long-serving colleagues. At the core of all provision, however, should be learning and the drive to improve teaching and learning for students, whatever forms the professional learning may take.

In many cases, professional learning will need to be placed in the context of the job role carried out by the person. Whatever the job role, lecturer, teacher, financial administrator, librarian, pastoral head, classroom assistant, some of the learning may need to be directed at the specific functions carried out by staff. While it is important to develop a wide range of expertise, each member of staff will require professional development that is job-specific. CPD, in the form of training, as defined earlier, may be needed to develop the specific skills required for a particular job role. Bradshaw and Farrell (2002) described the professional development required for assistants supporting children with severe learning difficulties, and they refer to the uniqueness of the role and how important it is in preparing for the role to differentiate it from the teacher's or careworker's, even though all the individual members of staff have to operate as a team and work with the same children. Best (2000), in a large-scale study of deputy headteachers' perceptions of their professional development, found that a significant majority most valued the support aimed at deputy headship, compared with more generic training about leadership and management. One of the key components of specific-role-based development is that it can raise the value which the post-holder places on the work they are doing. In addition, professional development of one group of staff can lead to other members of staff having a more positive view of the work they carry out, (see Naylor [1999] on mid-day assistants and Groom [2006] on teaching assistants). External validation is also likely to increase the value placed on the professional development by those in receipt of it.

In England, and also in other European countries (Karstanje, 2000), there has been a shift away from a focus on individual staff development to an increased emphasis on the system as a whole and each individual institution. The intention set out in the Schools White Paper (DfE, 2010) to establish a national network of teaching schools in the United Kingdom as part of a policy to develop a self-improving school system is an initiative designed to enable schools to work together to share effective practice. School leaders are intended to have the increased power and control to push through improvement across the system. Hargreaves (2010) set out a vision for the creation of self-improving schools including the establishment of school clusters, the development of local solutions, a need for co-operative working and the importance of system leaders. In subsequent 'think-pieces', he has developed the dynamics of an effective interschool partnerships and the development of a maturity model (Hargreaves, 2012a,b). An early example of this type of locally based mutual professional support system was researched by Abbott et al. (2012) who investigated a Primary School Improvement Project, based on staff from outstanding schools supporting colleagues in less successful schools and 'all heads referred to staff development as a key factor arising out of the work of the partnership. This took many forms:

- joint staff training across both schools, sometimes with outside speaker/trainer; sometimes joint training days have occurred

- staff from supporting school coming in to lead sessions

- staff from supported school shadowing colleagues in partner schools

- staff from supported school observing lessons in partner school

- staff from both schools sharing pupils' work for assessment or moderation
- reviews of staff such as subject leaders being carried out by the other school
- staff in similar roles "paired" or "buddied" across the two schools
- staff of both schools being involved in cluster training
- senior staff from both schools doing joint observation'.

(Abbott et al., 2012: 7)

There are five broad categories into which professional development can be categorized:

- Studying and analysing one's work including reflecting in both single- and double-loop terms upon one's own practice, and perhaps undertaking a systematic analysis of a process undertaken, as proposed by Brighouse (1991) who speculates why this microanalysis is so little employed in education compared to other professions such as medicine.

- Learning from other staff includes all everyday opportunities to talk with other colleagues, both more or less experienced than oneself. It also includes informal observations both in one's own school or college and when visiting, for whatever reason, other organizations.

- Specific provision including the processes and structures provided by the school or college, ranging from being mentored, appraised or formally observed to being given the opportunity to participate in decision-making or understudying a particular post for a period. This is in addition to seminars, workshop, conferences or structured visits which may be provided.

- External provision. Despite the emphasis on site-based provision as described above, it is still important for staff to meet and discuss with staff from other schools or colleges, so that an insular attitude is avoided and the widest source of ideas is accessed. In many countries external provision is supported by higher education institutions, who offer Masters level qualifications or the opportunity for further research though doctorate programmes.

- Personal reading and study.

Later chapters of this book will describe and examine some of the precise forms that actual provision can take and propose how each can be effective depending on the prior research that has been carried out concerning appropriateness.

Issues relating to provision of effective professional learning and CPD

As noted above, the priorities for any education system will vary from country to country; although it is probably true to say that economic improvement and viability is a prime consideration for ALL countries in the twenty-first century. A United Nations Report (1997), in pointing out that many millions of children in the world still do not have access to elementary education, and paying tribute to many remarkable teachers in the Third World, underlines how reasonable it is in some countries to place priority on actually getting children – and teachers – into schooling, rather than on more elaborate strategies for improving measurable performance. In such developing countries, a system at national level is essential and certain forms of training for teachers are inevitably applied 'across the board', in order to ensure equity for all children. After the formation of the new Republic of South Africa in 1994, the educational objective became to establish Curriculum 2005 (known as C2005) and introduce 'outcomes-based education'. Regardless of the merits and demerits of this, it necessitated a huge programme of national training for teachers, all committed to the same approach. According to critics, such as Jansen (2003), this has the effect of reducing teachers to facilitators and even craftspeople. Similarly, in Africa's smallest nation-state, the Seychelles, any new initiative is funnelled down from national to school level and the training involved has to be uniform. Heystek (2007) has described this kind of training as a form of 'moulding'.

In developed countries, there is considerable diversity of practice and the traditional strength of the teaching professions – and unions – can be a factor in the extent to which it may be possible to apply CPD across an education system. In the Netherlands, for example, the tradition of teachers' professional freedom as to whether they participate in CPD activities or not has posed problems for school leaders (Karstanje, 2000). In highly centralized systems, such as in Greece, the risk is that in rural areas distant from the government urban centres, any directives are ignored, with teachers safe in the knowledge that there is little likelihood of repercussions (see Middlewood, 2001: 14). It is also interesting to note that these two countries, as with several others, have a very considerable and influential sector of private schooling, which may be under no obligation to follow specified state policies in training and staff development.

We earlier noted the move towards greater organizational autonomy in many developed countries and tensions will therefore be likely to develop between national demands and individual school or college provision. In England and Wales, teachers once tended to choose their CPD activities in a relatively haphazard way (Collinson, 2008), but the introduction of a national curriculum led, in the 1990s, to a great deal of universal training

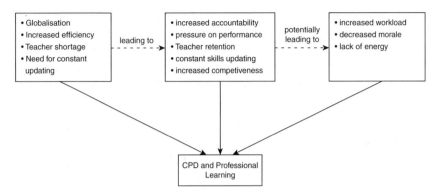

FIGURE 1.2 *External influences on CPD/professional learning.*

to implement this. Since greater 'marketization' of schools, a consequence has been the emergence of a plethora of private providers of training, offering everything from 'futureproofing' to 'performance life coaching' to 'Leading school improvement solutions' (see Ball, 2008: 195). Across 5 European countries and 700 primary headteachers, 25 per cent identified 'promoting professional development' as a significant problem (Bolam et al., 2000: 28). Such issues and potential tensions need school and college leaders to be aware of them and to address them in considering provision of effective staff development. In practice, there will be a number of factors outside the control of individuals or schools and colleges that influence professional learning in all its forms. These will range from broad issues such as globalization to the more narrow concerns of increased workloads. Figure 1.2 illustrates the major external influences on professional learning and CPD.

Identifying and meeting the needs of staff and students

If we reflect on why some CPD provision is seen as ineffective by its recipients, the views of writers such as Craft (1996), Blandford (2000), Earley and Bubb (2004), Bell and Bolam (2010) and Bush and Middlewood (2013) might be summarized broadly as it being perceived as:

- at the wrong time
- not specific to context
- in the wrong form
- irrelevant to some or all of the recipients.

While context has already been discussed, the last two of these are fundamental to the effectiveness of any activity planned to promote staff learning. If we consider the form that such activities may take, it is clear that theories of learning, especially adult learning, tell us that people learn in different ways and additionally, as adults, may be less flexible in their ability or willingness to try new forms. It is not sufficient for school and college leaders to recognize the importance of learning and to be certain that every individual is capable of it, but they will also need to take positive action to encourage people to take steps – especially first steps – to do something about it! In any context, some adults will lack confidence in their ability to learn new skills or knowledge and some fear failure in a new venture especially if they had not been involved in any professional learning activities for some time. This might be especially true of some support staff in schools and colleges. However, there is ample evidence of how support staff in particular roles have made a huge contribution to their organizations through their own learning, whether special needs assistant (Middlewood et al., 1998), school caretaker (Middlewood et al., 2005), office staff (Middlewood and Parker, 2009) and teaching assistants (Emira, 2011; Attwood and Bland, 2012). Leaders of effective learning schools or colleges will probably also want to explore ways in which teachers or lecturers who are on temporary or fixed-term contracts or come in to substitute for absent staff, are given opportunities for new learning to develop skills. It is important for any organization to identify and attempt to meet the needs of all such staff – and this includes carefully taking into account the form of provision to which a particular staff will most readily respond.

The other important factor, and one which will most readily 'switch off' people from any provision will be that of irrelevance. 'I could not see that it had anything to do with me!' would be the most damning of comments, because it represents time-wasting and probably boredom to very busy people. We strongly argue, therefore, that the identification of the specific needs – of individuals, of teams and of the organization – is perhaps the key element in providing professional learning which is seen as relevant and thereby meaningful for their work and an improvement for recipients.

Needs have to be identified at various levels throughout the school or college. We believe that essentially these are at:

- the individual level;
- the team level, such as subject area, department, year, leadership, or even a working group;
- the whole school or college level.

Unless each and all of these needs are addressed, relevance and motivation will be limited and of course, it is the role of the leaders and managers of staff learning to try to facilitate the way in which these cohere. This will be shown in later chapters, including through specific case examples of effective practice.

Since a learning school or college will necessarily be constantly questioning and challenging its own practices and processes in order to improve them, its provision of learning for staff will reflect this. For any improvement to be valid, it needs to be based on an authentic enquiry or research. Sometimes, this research can be carried out by a person external to the organization, but there is a considerable growth in several countries and interest in the organization carrying out its own investigations through some form of practitioner research; see, for example, Middlewood and Abbott (2012). This is done sometimes by the provision of Masters level programmes based in the schools or colleges themselves (Middlewood et al., 1998), or by staff, accessing these universities' programmes (Taysum, 2010). It is critical that all research carried out in and for the organization is of a high standard, using professional methodologies and following ethical procedures. One principal of a college with a high incidence of in-house research wrote that 'by becoming a research-engaged school, it has benefited enormously in that we have established a culture where all those working in the school have the opportunity and the means to question, evaluate and enrich the quality of the service that is being provided' (Parker, 2011: 83).

We believe strongly that such a culture should include the notion and practice of 'student voice'. If the shared values in this culture are really to be all-pervading, the omission of those people in the organization who are ultimately the receivers of the impact of staff learning makes no sense. A number of schools and colleges involve students not only in their in-house research, the majority at secondary and post-compulsory level, but also in a growing number of primary schools. The strongest argument for this in terms of developing a learning community is that the students or pupils, when given an opportunity to engage in debates about learning (based on their research), very readily become partners in the process rather than mere recipients. When professional practice is located 'in authentic student voice', it is able to be 'constantly redefined in terms of what it means to be a teacher today' (Kidd, 2012: 127).

Such experiences – of practitioner and of student in-house research – have been hugely successful and made a considerable impact on teaching, learning and management practice in some schools and colleges. Changes in practice need to be supported by new and relevant professional learning, and so it follows that in-house research which identifies a need for change or reinforcement, can be effectively used to identify areas which individuals or teams will find relevant in provision of professional learning. In later chapters, we explore in detail how this research can be carried out by staff and students to the greatest effect and how this can enable the opportunity to provide professional learning, which is relevant, and in the form which is most appropriate to the staff.

The aim for any organization ultimately is, as noted earlier, to develop a culture of shared values about learning and the processes we describe can contribute hugely to this. There is evidence that this will include celebrating success in learning and school, and college leaders will find the means of acknowledging and celebrating learning achievement in all kinds of ways. Ultimately, as Holyoke et al. (2011: 439) suggest, 'It is the cultural norms that define the effectiveness of the learning', and several of these features are found in the 'unique nature of education as compared to business and industry' (McCharen et al., 2011: 689).

The impact of professional learning and the evaluation of effective professional learning, including cost-effectiveness

With increasing competition for scarce resources within education, it is becoming even more important to consider whether professional learning activities are actually effective. In many cases, this is difficult to do because the activity often relates to the individual and impact is often spread over a long period. It has been proposed in fact that an indicator of successful learning organizations in the future may be 'the numbers of those inspired to become leaders themselves' (Slater, 2008: 67). Effective professional learning will impact on the individual, organization and the system as a whole. For an individual this may take a number of forms ranging from improved classroom performance to successful school or college leadership. For an organization, improvements in the quality of the staff should lead to improved teaching and learning. For the system as a whole to be effective, professional learning could contribute to improved staff recruitment and increased retention of key staff who will remain in the education sector.

Middlewood (1997) put forward a model for the evaluation of the effectiveness of staff development programmes but in practice, there has been no systematic attempt to do this. The following are questions which can act as possible indicators of progress made towards creating a more effective learning school or college over a period of time:

- Are meetings given over to debate about learning rather than operational issues?
- Are more staff using libraries and resource centres?
- Are more staff making better use of web-based resources?
- Are more staff offering to lead discussions?
- Are staff acknowledging the role of other agents in the learning role, for example, parents?

- Are staff willing to identify and acknowledge mistakes (their own and others') as learning experiences?
- Are the barriers to creativity in learning and teaching being recognized?
- Are the learning capabilities of *all* staff being recognized and being acted upon?
- Are different learning styles for staff being recognized in their own learning?
- Are *all* staff having the opportunities to formalize their learning achievements, if they wish to do so, and what proportion are actually doing so?
- Are more staff involved in research projects?
- Are more staff using self-evaluation exercises or reviews?
- Are more staff involved in working collaboratively, especially across subject areas and across institutions?
- Are more celebrations of learning success taking place?
- Is more in-house research taking place?

(Based on Middlewood et al. [2005] and Bush and Middlewood [2013])

These indicators do not address the other significant issue that concerns government about raising educational standards. Spending public money on education is often justified through the desire to drive up education standards. A focus on increased professional learning is often viewed by the government as a means of raising standards of student outcomes by improving the quality of the staff employed. It is an easy logic that a teaching profession that has had good initial preparation and on going professional development should be actually better at doing their fundamental job! Certainly, in England the Government recognized this with the publication of a White Paper interestingly titled 'The Importance of Teaching' (DfE, 2010). The prime minister and deputy prime minister claimed: 'The first and foremost lesson is that no education system can be better than the quality of its teachers . . . the second lesson of world-class education systems is that they devolve as much power to the front line, whilst retaining high levels of accountability' (Cameron and Clegg, 2010: 3–4).

Conclusion

It is unimaginable that in a sector devoted to learning there should not be a strong emphasis on learning for the staff who are employed in the sector. It is reasonable to ask, if education cannot provide appropriate opportunities for professional learning then which sector can? Creating a learning culture which supports the continual learning of all staff should be an aspiration of every school and college. There should be high expectations of professional learning and any CPD provision on the part of staff and leaders in schools and colleges to facilitate improvements in teaching and learning. Staff should be supported to develop evaluative skills, to discuss issues relating to teaching and learning, with time for observation, reflection and productive feedback. Research (BERA, 2014) should be at the heart of this process in ensuring that the professional learning and CPD provision is relevant and appropriately given; the emphasis should be on development, and opportunities for staff to identify their own needs and participate in critical reflection are crucial. As part of this process, performance management should help staff to identify their own learning needs for their development and also allow managers to provide opportunities for ongoing professional development in the way specified above.

While in many countries there is high-quality professional learning and CPD available to the full range of staff, there are still wide variations between countries and often between individual schools and colleges. Too often, it is still the case that factors such as the availability of sufficient funding, and the priority attached to professional learning and CPD by headteachers and principals are key factors in determining whether staff will have access to high-quality provision. Poor experience of professional learning and CPD opportunities or negative views of experienced staff can all contribute to a failure to develop a culture that is supportive of significant staff development. In some cases there is also too much emphasis on specific training (sometimes dictated by national requirements) at the expense of the development of a truly relevant learning organization.

The best schools and colleges do succeed in becoming learning organizations and there has to be an expectation that staff will continue to learn and develop throughout their working lives. This has to become integral to the way in which the organization operates in what is an ever-changing and complex world. For continual improvement in teaching and learning to take place, more systems and schools and colleges will have to accept and develop the characteristics of a learning organization – and effective professional learning and development lies at the heart of this.

These themes are of course developed in detail in later chapters. The way in which research-based enquiry can be central to a school or college's development is examined in Chapter Two and how this is linked to the concept of the whole organization and its learning needs is shown later in Chapter Six. These two chapters and the others of the first six chapters show how effective in-house research can significantly aid relevant and meaningful provision of professional learning or CPD. As the extended case studies in the following chapters clearly demonstrate, there are some schools and colleges that have discovered this already.

Summary of Chapter One

This chapter has:

- defined the meaning of professional learning and CPD and suggested key purposes,

- explained its importance in school and college development,

- described the importance of developing a culture of effective professional learning and CPD,

- discussed the various forms of professional learning and CPD provision,

- discussed some of the issues facing managers of professional learning and CPD provision,

- stressed the importance of needs identification and linked this with in-house research and

- briefly reflected on outcomes and evaluation of professional learning and CPD.

CHAPTER TWO

The school/college as a research-based community

Introduction

Having explored the significance of professional learning in various forms and linked it to developing improved practice, it is important to examine how inquiry processes within the school or college can be one of the most effective means to achieve this. This chapter therefore:

- stresses the importance of organizational self-evaluation,

- describes the value of internal practitioner research,

- proposes the principles for effective practitioner research,

- emphasizes the need for working collaboratively and how this can develop into a research-based professional learning community and

- discusses the potential barriers to achieving this and some strategies to overcome these.

The importance of organizational self-evaluation

We should state at the outset that there is quite clearly, both in accountability and the ensuring of high achievement, a definite place for some form of EXTERNAL evaluation; all countries we are aware of have some form of this, in terms of inspection processes. The value of these lies in their objectivity, brought to bear by those who are not involved in the normal procedures of an organization. These inspections are often done by government agencies, although in some countries, notably those with autonomous or semi-autonomous educational institutions, such services are often deemed to be independent of national governments, in case political 'interference' is seen to be present.

This kind of inspection can be summarized as 'an external, summative process, judging the extent to which an organization meets externally imposed criteria' (West-Burnham, 1994: 158) and as such, clearly has limitations. Many inspection systems themselves (e.g. in England and Wales, New Zealand, Australia, Seychelles, Canada) recognize this by including assessments of how effective the school or college is in its own evaluation of itself. In these cases, schools and colleges are asked to complete a formal self-evaluation process, which is then studied as part of the external inspection.

Compared with inspection, self-evaluation can be seen as 'an internal, formative process designed to give feedback on the total impact or value of a project or activity' (ibid.: 158). This will usually involve monitoring, and the focus of any such self-evaluation will clearly depend upon the institution's key values and purposes; any identified issues can then be addressed – and successes celebrated – through relevant action. Briggs neatly summarizes the blending of the two processes by saying that:

> Over a period of time, performance – and success – will be judged both externally and internally, in formative ways which enable future direction to be determined, and in summative ways which may place a 'snapshot' judgement, fixed in time. (Briggs, 2002: 182)

This statement understandably presupposes that this is how the two processes, external and internal, 'should' coalesce to support development. However, in the early decades of the twenty-first century, with a huge emphasis on international comparisons via published attainment league tables, educational institutions are often pressured in this so-called performativity culture to conform to external criteria demands, almost always measurable ones in terms of test or examination results. This can mean for schools and colleges which wish to encourage their children and young people to be effectively prepared for this century's needs, in terms of both citizenship and economic prosperity, a potential clash of priorities or imperatives. While external demands may appear to require competition, hierarchy and control for example, the community and environmental needs may appear to be more sympathetic to collaboration, networks, trust and interdependence. Thus, internal self-evaluation with a formative intention is a crucial component in the ongoing development of any organization which wishes to strive for continuing progress, and in the case of schools and colleges, for the continuing improvement in their students' learning.

Internal investigation into practice

Because the focus of a school or college is on learning, the self-evaluation clearly needs to be on that learning, and the teaching and other factors that enable effective learning. Only by regularly reassessing internal practices can improvement occur, and since it seems clear that effective learning of pupils and students can only occur when teachers and lecturers are themselves effective learners, then it is in this area that the constant emphasis must be placed. Since the concept of lifelong learning for effective teachers (Day, 1999) is now widely accepted, the question for schools and colleges striving for improvement, is how they can encourage and develop professional learning. If this can lead to the establishment of what is called a professional learning community, through collaboration and reflection, then effective practice and improvement is almost certain. (Katzenmeyer and Moller, 2001; Timperley, 2011). In a twenty-year longitudinal research study, comparing improving and declining schools, Bryk et al. (2010) found that focusing on student learning and professional capacity (developing teachers' learning) were two of the 'ingredients' most crucial to school success. They also noted however that, without trust, no list of ingredients could succeed, as it is what transforms initiatives for change into the climate within which real change can occur. The point here is that trust is essentially an organizational internal feature which we believe is earned through collaboration between members who 'own' the initiatives and not something which is a kind of 'blind faith' in criteria imposed by an external body. In simple human terms, given certain conditions, we tend to trust those we know before those we do not know!

But what is the best way of finding out what the areas are, for improvement in practice to support professional learning? We believe that finding out in a systematic and properly conducted manner the true experiences of learning (and teaching, therefore) within the school or college is the most effective way – in other words, through carrying out internal practitioner research. We believe this to be so because:

CONTEXT is all important. Although there are key principles in effective learning and teaching, CPD and research, each school or college is unique and research has indicated how 'context-specific' therefore is the application of any initiative. 'One size fits all' is simply not an option, because of the special features of each individual culture which exists in the institution. Looking at effective practice elsewhere and considering whether it could work here or adapting it is clearly sensible, but the wholesale transplanting of approaches is very unlikely to succeed. In our own context, we are able to see what works and what does not.

INSIDER INFLUENCE is more powerful than that of an outsider. As noted above, there IS a place for external input, but human nature recognizes that we prefer to do something if we have found the need for it ourselves, rather than being told by somebody else! Teachers for example, are mostly proudly independent professionals and want to make their own changes in their classroom practice. Therefore, examination of this practice – and that of their colleagues – is likely to be taken notice of more carefully than that of an outside expert, however good. Research into practitioner research itself has found that even teachers' understanding of their own subject can be enhanced by this. For example, D'Ambrosio (1998: 146) found that mathematics teachers discovered, through in-house research 'even more about student understanding of mathematics, mathematics itself', as well as about themselves as teachers. The history of teachers' research into their own classroom practice (action research) was based firmly on this principle of discovering about one's own practice. Many good practices which support learning from colleagues have a part to play in developing professional learning. Examples include shadowing, mentoring, observation, learning walks. However, there are limitations to all forms of learning in-house. When practitioners are keen to learn, and often short of time as well, it is tempting to observe a more skilled person in action, for example, and have a natural instinct to see whether what we saw can be transferred to work with 'our own classes'. But just as transplanting practice wholesale from one country to another is extremely risky, so it is wrong to assume that the cross classroom transplant will work, if one does not take account of the very rich experience that the skilled practitioner has previously worked through.

The other particular reason why colleagues' in-house research can be respected compared with external is the sheer authenticity of it. As one practitioner noted, 'The many journals, books and research by education theorists are undoubtedly useful, but I sometimes wonder: do they have exercise books, assessments, course work and mock exams to mark? Action Plans to write? Grades to meet? Staff teams to build in school? Teachers who research inherently often build these into their own research' (Capstick, 2013: 14).

DISSEMINATION of the findings from research is a good deal easier within a school or college when the actual research has been carried out there and colleagues have usually been involved. Where they are involved, they will have given permission for it to be done and have a built-in interest in the results. Structures and general arrangements for dissemination are established straightforwardly and can be readily used. The normal communication processes within the place can be used and the discussion of the findings therefore readily enabled.

IMPLEMENTATION OF RECOMMENDATIONS is much more likely if these come from internal research, following an agreed process. If recommendations are not accepted and/ or implemented, there can be vigorous debate and the potential implementers will be expected to explain the reasons for non-implementation. These of course may be excellent reasons, but the debate itself about them is bound to be useful in airing the whole topic which was under investigation.

EVALUATION OF ANY CONSEQUENT CPD may be also more useful where the original reasons for the provision of the CPD sprang from agreed internal research processes. The whole area of evaluating CPD is a difficult and sometimes contentious one. Guskey (1995: 117–18) has suggested that 'it is impossible to make precise statements about the elements of an effective professional development programme'. Since any such programmes here will have been undertaken for a very specific purpose, following a research-based identification of a learning need, it is more likely that the evaluation can be much more specific about how well that need was met and demonstrated in subsequent practice. The consequences of the impact (or non-impact!) of a CPD programme identified in this way will be evident in the school or college in a visible way – much more so than the conventional formal course signed up for in a general sense of wanting to improve.

Principles for effective practitioner research

We need to state at the outset, that there are clear principles that should be applied in any kind of research – whoever is carrying it out and wherever it is applied. We suggest that these should include the belief that all research should:

- be honest and use an ethically based approach throughout;
- have a clearly stated purpose;
- use the research instruments that are appropriate for the stated purpose;
- analyse the findings objectively;
- come to conclusions based on the actual findings;
- make any recommendations based on the actual findings;
- recognize the limitations of the research;
- enable the researcher(s) to learn from the process and do even better next time.

Unless such principles as these are adhered to, it will be possible for some to question the validity of the findings, and therefore be reluctant to follow any recommendations based on them.

For practitioner research to be effective – and we have stated the advantages earlier – it is also important to recognize that there are potential disadvantages to be aware of. These could include the following:

- It may be more difficult to maintain objectivity in a context which you know well and in which you inevitably have some vested interests.

- You may come under direct or indirect pressure at some point, for example in choosing a particular topic, or – much worse – to present findings in a particular way which reflects someone else's preference.

- Conflicts of interest may arise during the research, which may involve personal loyalties.

- Some of the findings generated may cause personal problems, either because they relate to your own practice or they affect those with whom you have personal relationships.

Each of these potential disadvantages stresses the complete need for the first principle stated above, that the research must be honest and follow an ethically based approach throughout. Only in this way can personal issues be risen above or put aside. Once this has been firmly established as the norm in the organization, then colleagues come to accept that there is nothing personal in the research or its findings, but it is all part of an overall attempt to achieve personal, professional and institutional improvement. This ethical approach is the first of our principles for effective practitioner research and the following should be noted carefully:

- All participation in in-house research is voluntary and nobody has to be involved if they do not want to be. What is known as 'informed consent' has to be obtained from anyone whom you wish to be the subject of the research. This means that they agree to take part and they know exactly what it is that they have agreed to.

- Confidentiality must be respected. All data collected about and from respondents are given in confidence and can only be used as agreed by the parties at the start. Such data can only be used for the purpose for which they were collected; this is in any case a legal requirement in most countries. Strictly speaking, the data collected belong to the person or persons from whom they were obtained.

- Anonymity is sometimes more difficult to preserve in in-house practitioner research because the need to disguise identity is as crucial as ever, but, especially in a small school for example, where 'everyone knows everyone else', it may be almost impossible. However, real names must not be used and the best plan is to refer to research subjects by role, such as teacher A or teaching assistant B. In specific cases, such as the principal/headteacher or the head of a particular subject department, it will be obvious to readers from inside the institution whose identity it is, but the objectivity should be maintained by the person being referred to as 'The principal' or 'HoD' on all occasions.

- Privacy is also crucial. Interviews, for example, should be conducted where they cannot be overheard and the data collected must not become a source of informal discussion or 'chat' with anyone outside the research group.

- Sensitivity needs also to be shown. The research should not be too intrusive into people's personal lives and the subject's own time and circumstances should be respected. These are colleagues that you have to work with on a daily basis after the research is finished!

- Finally, it should be checked whether the particular school or college has any specific data – holding regulations – and the national ones checked also of course. There is normally a set period beyond which data collected for any specific purposes must not be retained, and should be destroyed. It is essential that this is done, unless very specific permission is obtained – in writing – from the person or persons affected.

(Note that specific practitioner research practice is returned to in Chapter Six when we examine inquiring into individual classroom practice.)

Choosing the topic and being clear about purpose

The topic for research may be determined by personal identification, by discussion with colleagues or a senior person, by reference to a school or college official priority; however it is chosen, it is essential in our view that it is something in which the person has a genuine interest. It seems obvious, but without that interest, personal and/or professional, there may be little motivation to act upon any proposals arising from the inquiry. Middlewood and Abbott (2012: 16) suggest that a topic should avoid being too broad, too trivial or too technical.

It is also essential that there should be a clear and specific purpose to the research, in effect to answer the question, 'What are we trying to find out?' See Case Example 2A for an illustration.

CASE EXAMPLE 2A

A VERY SPECIFIC PURPOSE

Joe taught English to a group of 16–17-year-olds in a Further Education College in South West England, trying to get them to achieve a GCSE. The boys in the class were easily bored and very uninterested in reading, most of them rarely doing the reading required outside of lessons. Joe had tried various new ways of getting them interested through e-texts and DVDS, but it was not until he developed a clear piece of structure investigation that he made a breakthrough. Agreed with an in-house tutor, the research question was 'To what extent can use of non-conventional methods help male students improve their English reading attainment?'

The boys were divided into three simple groups:

(1) Facebook was used to develop discussion forums, linking with specific reading texts.
(2) Audio-books were used with a small sample.
(3) The third group were taught conventionally, including sessions of quiet reading.

All groups volunteered for a specific group. Questionnaires and interviews were used to get feedback.

Joseph found that 'I was surprised that both the first two groups responded so keenly. I was especially surprised that the audio books were seen as so accessible by the boys, as they broke books into manageable chunks. The social network sites seemed to give those boys an effective way to revise texts for exams. The bonus was that the previously most disaffected boys used the sites most and most boys said they read more than previously. There was a large increase in boys achieving or surpassing target grades, but I noted that the conventional methods still worked well for those choosing them. There's a place for all of these, and it's surely horses for courses!'

Reading

Reading is in any case a major source of professional learning and practitioners need to do some background reading before embarking on the research.

It is not our intention here to describe all the technical aspects of carrying out the actual research. We have already written about this in detail elsewhere (Middlewood and Abbott, 2012) and would refer both leaders and practitioners to that; in addition, Chapter Five of this book describes the practicalities of carrying out the research, in terms of methods and sampling. However, some important points do need stressing.

Type of research and research design

Practitioners often have a preference for quantitative or qualitative research, sometimes according to their specialist subject areas, but usually in-house research involves a mixture of both. Some basic reading about at least the two key research paradigms, positivist and interpretivist, is helpful but it is important not to become bogged down with elitist research terminology.

Analysing the findings data

Depending on the nature of the data, the analysis will vary. However, it should remain simple, if only because great complexity rarely leads to straightforward action and this is what is being looked for here. For example, analysis of quantitative data does not require more than descriptive statistics, and qualitative data can often be analysed in terms of themes. Many researchers prefer the word 'discussion' to 'analysis' in this context and it is possible that this will appear less intimidating to the person being researched.

Conclusions and recommendations

Conclusions are not just a way of 'rounding off' the findings. They enable the researchers(s) to step back and reflect on what may be found from the whole thing. Some statements therefore are needed about what can be reasonably deduced from the whole process. Therefore, the conclusions should:

- remind everyone for whom the report is intended;
- return to the original purpose of the research;
- ensure that everything in the conclusions can be referred back to evidence in the findings.

The recommendations section of a report is also brief and can easily be presented in a few bullet-point statements. Again, one should remember for whom the recommendations are made and they need to be:

- realistic and practical,
- probably involve relatively small changes,
- have an understanding of what resources may be involved,
- perhaps include some element of reflection, consideration by the research object.

Validity and limitations

We suggested earlier that good research always offers opportunities for the researcher to learn how to do better next time. The first step in this is for the researcher to reflect on whether the findings are properly valid and whether there are any limitations that should be noted about the process and/or the findings, affecting the conclusions and thereby recommendations.

Validity can be seen in the in-house context as mainly relating to the proper nature of the research process. Thus the researcher needs to reflect whether the correct procedures were followed, ethically and technically. Was the sample adequate? Were the methods appropriate? Were the instruments piloted? Was the inquiry carried out at the right time? These are all technical questions, but the researcher(s) also need to reflect on whether their own personal values and judgements have in any way unintentionally distorted the findings and discussion, or whether the overall institutional need for a specific outcome has influenced the process. Any reservations that might exist about any of these should be recognized and acknowledged in the writing up of the report. Middlewood and Abbott (2012: 115) give such an example (adapted):

> While the sample of interviews cannot be claimed to represent the full range of – in the college, the researcher believes the data gives a sufficient picture of attitudes within this staff level for conclusions to be drawn. The researcher has made every effort to ensure that his own position in the college has not influenced his ability to be objective.

Presenting the report

The first person or persons to whom the report should be given is the object(s) of the research. This is a matter of professional courtesy and also offers them a final chance to peruse it for accuracy and fairness. We would advocate then a period for those concerned for reflection on what the report says. It is easy to talk of the reflective practitioner so this is where the value of reflection can be shown. Reflecting helps us to understand the links between feeling, thinking and action. Our feelings affect how we think and this affects what we do. For the practitioner who has volunteered to have their practice put under scrutiny, this can be the most important time.

'What is this telling me about what I do?'

'Do I have to change a little or a lot?'

'How does this affect me as a person?'

'Can I actually do what is suggested here?'

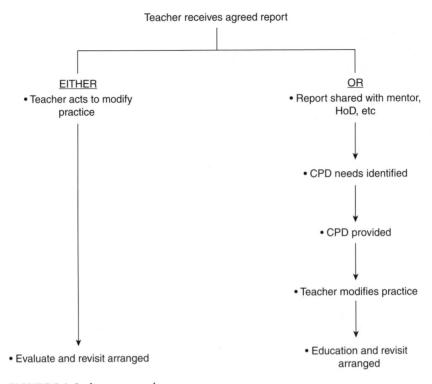

FIGURE 2.1 *In-house procedure.*

'If I do accept the suggestions, what help do I need, and where and how do I get that help?'

These may be some of the questions to be asked in self-reflection, before the report goes forward to the appropriate body. These may be at middle or senior level in a school or college and, if a research community is to be a meaningful one, the leadership level is probably essential. At the very least, a simple model can operate as shown in Figure 2.1.

Dissemination and implementation

How far the dissemination is made depends upon the institution's culture and practice, the consent originally given by the participants and of course upon the recommendations. These will have been carefully considered by the relevant body which has the authority to implement them. If they only concern a particular individual's practice, then fewer people will be involved, as in Figure 2.1. The issue of resources will be considered by the relevant person and action proposed accordingly, as Case Example 2B shows:

CASE EXAMPLE 2B

IDENTIFYING A 'WEAK SPOT'

An in-house practitioner inquiry had resulted in identifying for Glenda, an English Teacher of four years' experience in an academy in London, that her poetry lessons were the least successful. While her enthusiasm for, and knowledge of, poetry was high, her students found her poetry lessons 'irrelevant' and often 'boring', unlike most of her other ones. A recommendation that she should 'seek further advice or relevant CPD', she found only partly helpful, as no formal CPD programmes seemed appropriate.

Discussion with the Head of Department led to her attending an after-school music club 'to see another side to her students', run by a new music teacher. The club involved the students choosing their own music and also having a go at writing their own raps or songs. 'I felt really out of it,' Glenda said, 'and rather embarrassed when they asked me to join in!' However, she was very struck by the students' total involvement with the words and the rhythms.

'In a subsequent poetry lesson', I began by asking them to write something in whatever form they wanted – verse, or rap, or even a speech – on broadly, the violence of war theme. They produced some lively material, which we shared and commented on. For my turn, I offered Owen's 'Anthem for Doomed Youth', which they accepted as my choice and commented on accordingly. They loved it! They savoured the words and the rhythms of, I remember especially – 'the stuttering rifles' rapid rattle'. They recognized too that it was the poet's own experience. My learning? In no way is this 'going down with the kids! My own love of poetry is undiminished but I don't assume now, because I the teacher like it, you should appreciate it. I regularly look for the students' insights. Great literature speaks to all of us, all ages, all eras, and my students and I can share this. We are just coming at it from our two different angles, but it means something to us both.

Developing a research-based learning community

However effectively the principles and practices described above are applied, they will not automatically lead to overall school or college improvement without the crucial presence of collaboration between practitioners. Without collaboration, there may be an institution of effective but isolated practitioners. As Day (1999) suggested, while a professional practitioner needs to reflect on their own practice, reflection on its own is not enough for organizational improvement. Staff need to share with each other their ideas and what they have learned and ultimately this leads to the development of what is often referred to as a professional learning community (PLC). In a school or college where in-house practitioner research is widespread and becoming the norm, a 'community of enquiry' (McGuigan, 2008: 11) is beginning to emerge. We believe that where the collaboration between colleagues is primarily based upon the sharing of the practice of practitioner research within the institution and its community then the resultant learning community will be extremely powerful. One of the extended case studies – described in Chapter Seven – is an example of the development of such a community.

We believe this because, as Nehring and Fitzsimons (2011: 63) pointed out, 'Teachers working together does not necessarily mean teachers working collaboratively.' In other words, they are not necessarily sharing. True collaboration involves working interdependently to analyse practice so that there can be improvement both individually and collectively. Each teacher or lecturer may have their own agenda and their own preferred practice; the in-house practitioner research enables them together to examine the findings and reconsider their original practice. Of course, there may often simply be reinforcement of good current practice but the sharing of the bases of this will be debated and shared, leading to clearer understanding. It is the reflection on the findings plus the sharing that leads to the professional learning. It is questions that drive learning, rather than easily available answers.

Inevitably, this process of building a collaborative learning community takes time, partly because change is a constant, especially in the educational world. Using new technologies is an obvious example in the twenty-first century where 'there are new dexterities to be learned and traditional dexterities need to be re-learned' (Woollard, 2012: 47).

Perhaps one of the key elements in sharing is simply to develop a 'culture of talk' (Fletton and Warwick, 2012: 114). This may involve:

Easy and effective communication by both voice and email but also by physical proximity of staff in the same collaborative teams:

- Opportunities for informal one-to-one and also group dialogue

- Time for staff to meet and talk in informal contexts

(Adapted from Carnell and Lodge [2002])

We should note that even in twenty-first-century times of instant electronic communication, staff have often been found to prefer face-to-face meetings to share through talking; as Widodo and Riandi (2013) found in their research in Indonesia; when even the most modern sophisticated 'e-talk' was offered, face-to-face contact was found to be nearly always 'the preferred mode' (ibid.: 388). Carnell (2001) found that the more people discovered about their learning, the more they wanted to talk about it, and the more they talked about it, the more they wanted to find out – a natural process!

The process is likely to be significantly more difficult and lengthy within an education system which is highly centralized and where institutions are used to receiving 'edicts from above' and simply applying them in a standard way. In these contexts, CPD is usually dealt with and delivered similarly, leaving very little – if any – scope for individual application. Bezzina (2008) mentions France, Spain, Greece, several African nations, some Asian ones and a number of East European countries in this context. However, we can refer to two examples, from Indonesia and Malta, where professional learning at institutional level may be emerging as a positive. Widodo and Riandi's (2013) research challenged the top-down model of CPD as a 'ritual' (ibid.: 389) and reported on attempts to build a learning community (ibid.: 388). Their recommendations were that only through teacher ownership of their own professional learning, aided by internal inquiry, could the Indonesian system prepare for the future effectively; acknowledging it will be a lengthy process.

In Malta, Bezzina (2008: 25) describes how the nurturing in a school of a culture of collaboration, challenged by internal inquiry 'is indeed difficult given that they were used to working on their own. The head reported that it 'has taken a lot of time and at times was quite tiring'. Ultimately, the community with its valuing of differences and disagreements, enabled people to see their dependence on each other and the collective value for the pupils, but only after 'a lot of hard work and sacrifice' (ibid.: 25).

What importance do actual leaders have in developing such research-based learning communities?

Leaders have an absolutely crucial role to play. In the final section of this chapter, we make specific recommendations for action, but here we can first note that in arguing for effective PLCs, Harris and Jones (2010: 174) noted that 'the quality of any system cannot outperform the quality of its leaders'. Honingh and Hodge's research (2014) and King (2011) showed that teachers were much more likely to engage in collaboration when they received support from their leaders, echoing Blase and Blase's major work of 2004 in the United States. Studies in Australia, and by the OECD (Organisation for Economic and Cultural Development) (Pont, 2008), have all reinforced the huge influence of leaders in the development of collaboration among educational professionals in building learning communities. This may take the form of providing time, creating the conditions and culture for teacher collaboration (King, 2011), or encouraging and supporting through personal interest and, perhaps above all, using the actual research outcomes to change the institution where it shows this to be for improvement.

Potential barriers to a research-based learning community and strategies to overcome these

We have noted above the amount of time it may need for such a community to be developed and here it is worth also considering a few other issues that may arise, and some possible approaches to addressing them.

- Staff may feel insecure, discomfited, even threatened if they wonder whether an in-depth inquiry into their own practice may expose inadequacies in, for example, their knowledge. This will make them very wary of being thus exposed (Huillet et al., 2001).

- There is a risk that teachers or lecturers will automatically prefer to see merit in other practice which is the most similar to their own (Smith and Engelson, 2012) and therefore be reluctant to accept evidence which suggests something very different. As Fullan (2001) pointed out, it is crucial that only good practice is reinforced by collaboration, so the recognition that the attitude of 'It works for me and for them, so why change?' may be a particularly difficult one to modify.

- Some staff have real misgivings about the relationships in the classroom or laboratories being damaged by detailed questions being asked about what is going on there.

- Some may feel that they will automatically be under pressure to accept all outcomes of any research and there will be little scope for disagreement with them.

- Some may simply feel that the whole process is a distraction – in a very busy professional life – to getting on with the daily tasks and procedures which they are under pressure to perform.

- Finally, even those who are reasonably supportive may be concerned that the school or college may become too inward looking and ignore the importance of linking with other institutions.

Overcoming these potential barriers

The simplest answer to most of these potential objections is for those who believe strongly in the great value of internal research and developing a learning community to just do it! Of course, this presupposes that a leader or leaders of the school or college is one who has that belief, because without their backing, success is unlikely. It is also essential, as we have previously stressed, that any such research is both professionally and ethically carried out. As with most initiatives, 'change agents' or 'change champions' are needed, as demonstrating success early on can be a great motivation for others to join. As Kanter (1988) stresses, given a champion – or two or three, all that may be needed then is time.

> There is a point in every fresh idea when discouragements mount and the temptation to stop is great . . . The inevitable problems, roadblocks and low spots are the critical hurdles in achieving a healthy return on the investment of time.

It is quite possible that an early piece of in-house practitioner research may suggest that a particular current practice is very good or requires only minor modification and even sceptics can be convinced in such circumstances, even if it does take the time that Kanter refers to! The crucial point is that participation is voluntary both by researchers and all respondents.

Because the role of the leaders is so important, we suggest that some of the following attitudes and actions will be helpful for them to consider in developing a culture essential for the research-based learning community.

- Be tolerant of learning through failure.

- Accept that disagreements are a good thing.

- Realize that a PLC can be challenging and even 'troublesome' or 'subversive' (Nehring and Fitzsimons, 2011).

- Ensure that facilities and resources are available (e.g. staff library) to support in-house research.

In terms of roles and structures:

- model the process though personal action;

- ensure that 'research and development' is in the job description of at least one senior leader in the school or college;

- ensure that all new staff recruited are keen on participation in in-house research and have an interest in research-based learning;

- establish a specific research and development group which coordinates the in-house research and encourages access to relevant reading;

- ensure that all job descriptions involve reference to research and evidence-based practice;

- ensure that if staff are released to attend external CPD, they are expected to know the research basis for whatever it entailed;
- perhaps establish a leadership research community, committed to researching and improving internal leadership and management practice.

To address the last of the potential barriers cited above, avoid insularity by:

- ensuring collaborative research with other schools or colleges, across local federations or chains, or families of schools,
- encourage research involving parents, local stakeholders such as employers, external agencies.

These last two relate to a need for careful timing, that is when the internal process is relatively well established.

Given these factors, the successful development of widespread practitioner research leading to a strong research-based professional learning community has tremendous potential. Not only can it fulfil the potential of all those involved as individual and collaborative learners, but this itself means that the school or college will be significantly placed to deliver real change, because it is based on what they exist for – the constant learning of those involved. However, for this community to be fully achieved, as Bush and Middlewood (2013: 236) note, 'If it is really to be an all pervading and true sharing of values, the omission of those people in the organisation who are ultimately the recipients of the impact of staff learning makes no sense.' The opportunity therefore for students and pupils to become partners in the process rather than mere recipients is essential and it is to this that we turn our attention in the next chapter.

Summary of Chapter Two

This chapter has:

- described the importance of self-evaluation for schools and colleges,
- explained the value of internal inquiries within them,
- proposed the principles and practice for effective practitioner research,
- stressed the significance of collaboration,
- emphasized how a learning community can be developed from this,
- suggested some potential barriers to successfully implementing this community and
- suggested some possible strategies for overcoming these barriers.

CHAPTER THREE

Involving learners in research and professional learning

The previous chapter dealt with how a school or college could develop as a 'research-engaged' institution by encouraging practitioner research on a wide scale. Through this, it could identify accurately the perceived needs of staff development, and manage and provide learning opportunities for them accordingly. In this chapter, we focus on the relevance of this approach to the actual students or pupils in the school or college and how they can also contribute to and gain from this. The chapter therefore:

- describes the growing interest in and importance of student voice,
- considers the purposes and benefits of student voice,
- stresses the importance of validity in student voice,
- proposes principles and practice for effective student research, and its relevance to professional learning,
- discusses the possible barriers to this and possible strategies for overcoming them and
- suggests ways in which student research may be initiated and developed.

(To avoid confusion, we use the term 'student voice' throughout this chapter to apply to pupils, students and learners of all ages.)

The emergence of student voice

In the conventional educational institution of the majority of the twentieth century, the role of the learner was essentially a passive one, with the effectiveness of the outcomes being dependent on the teacher 'giving' and the learner 'receiving'. Towards the later parts of that century, there were strong signs that the goal for the twenty-first century would be, in idealistic terms at least, the move from the 'teaching school to the learning school' (Middlewood et al., 2005: 32). In this context, the roles of both teacher and learner are significantly changed.

> Teachers are no longer all-knowing figures, full of unquestioned knowledge which they dispense. (Thomson, 2009: 674)

Inevitably, as much literature and indeed, much of this book stresses, the focus has been on how the shift not only affects the teacher/lecturer but also how the changes in that role and the expectations on it would bring about the change in educational processes. We use the word 'inevitably' because the need for the professionals in the teacher/learner relationship to change was paramount, if some of the various concerns for twenty-first-century educational effectiveness were to be faced and fulfilled.

With this effectiveness being expected to reveal itself in such elements as:

- individualized learning
- risk-taking and creativity
- flexibility
- team working
- resilience and perseverance
- learning from failure,

the teacher's role was shifting significantly. Added to this was the emergence of 'e-learning' and, in developed countries, the almost universal access to that knowledge and process as well as many different types of accessing learning.

However, in formal educational institutions such as schools and colleges, the emphasis to acknowledge the accompanying need for a change in the learner's role has been slower. Although it has been recognized within the teaching/learning situation, that is, the classroom, because clearly if teaching is different, so is the response to it, the recognition that the voice of the learner should be heard at different stages of education outside the classroom was, and many would claim, still is, very considerably lagging behind. Internationally, the learner had remained for the most part in a state of 'traditional powerlessness' (Lumby, 2001: 7), and Lumby suggested that in many countries the introduction of a market- or quasi-market approach to education had meant that, as in any business, educational providers had begun to see the need to listen to their consumers or customers to some extent. If the goals of twenty-first-century education have any chance of being achieved, there is surely a need for student or pupil involvement in the educational process.

What forms can student voice take? A broad definition could involve any way in which students are allowed to, or are invited to, discuss their views on their own education and the processes to which they are subject. A more precise one might suggest that it is about teachers becoming more attentive to what learners say about their experiences in the educational process. Student voice may be seen as about consultation, that is, taking students' views into account in reaching decisions about in-house processes. It could be seen as primarily about encouraging student participation in school or college matters. Beyond these broad definitions, it is necessary to examine purposes in more detail.

Purposes and benefits of student voice

It could be argued that the interest in student voice has been an inevitable development from the United Nations Convention on the Rights of the Child (1989), where Article 12 states that 'Children have the right to say what they think should happen when adults are making decisions that affect them, and to have their opinions taken into account.' In the United Kingdom, various pieces of legislation including The Children's Act of 1992 and more recently the Act of 2004 stipulated that the needs of young people and children should be recognized in local children's services and that they should be encouraged to be involved in the design and delivery of these services.

Others, such as Thomson (2009), argue that student voice may be simply recognition of the changing relationships between adults and children in twenty-first-century society, at least in western societies. As the notion of childhood has changed, with earlier biological maturity and recognition of earlier access to adult responsibilities, such as voting and consumer rights, so the 'one-way' emphasis in the power relationship with adults has shifted away from adults automatically speaking on behalf of children. Children and young people are therefore more likely to be expected to speak on their own behalf.

Others, such as Whitty and Wisby (2007), argue that student voice is ultimately about the democratization of educational institutions, where the rights of all those involved in the whole system operating there need to be recognized. It is about active citizenship which encourages children and young people to prepare for their fulfilling role in society at large through meaningful engagement while in formal education. They note that in

England and Wales the introduction of a specific citizenship element in the national curriculum in 2002 underlined the case for the voice of students to be heard in schools. Without a recognition of the value of having a voice in the community, it might be argued that young people emerge into society at large with a very limited concept of societal structures and their place within them.

It needs to be mentioned here that certain countries, of which the Nordic nations are probably the best example, have had the voice of students well established in their educational systems. Mortimore (2013: 206) points out that 'having the collective voice of the pupils supported by their student union – is one of the ways in which the next generation of citizens is introduced to democracy'. He notes that these voices are taken seriously – 'even by ministers' (ibid.: 232). This, we should also note, occurs in countries, such as Netherlands and Scandinavia, where the power of headteachers and principals is more limited than in many other countries, and where in some cases a head of subject or department may be elected to that office by their peers.

Others, including Flutter and Ruddock (2004), suggest that student voice may be particularly helpful in enabling those students disaffected with school or college life to understand that they have a legitimate place there and help to adjust their view of such places as being completely authoritarian with little or no relevance to their own needs. In discussing the 'direct' impact of student voice, Ruddock and McIntyre (2007) suggest that being consulted within a school can have a beneficial effect on the self-esteem of students and of these students especially in terms of their attitudes to school and classroom. Angus (2006) suggests that educational leaders have a moral responsibility to such disaffected students to generate student voice to engage them in an effort to avoid their disillusionment and even denigration by the establishment. Smyth (2006) also suggests that leaders are needed who will foster student voice so that many students from urban, ethnic minority and working-class backgrounds are not rejecting school or college as not for them.

Another perception of the significance of student voice is that it is an extension of leadership (Frost, 2008). With distributed leadership being the 'normatively preferred model of leadership' (Bush and Middlewood, 2013: 21), it is perfectly logical for that distribution to include the students in an educational institution. Since distributed leadership concentrates on engaging expertise wherever it exists rather than through formal position or role (Harris, 2008), the argument would be that there are no greater experts on educational processes than those who are the recipients of the effects of these.

Finally, and we place it here because it is the aspect on which we shall focus the most, student voice can be seen as having a powerful impact on teaching and learning, because of the unique perception that students have – as the direct recipients of teaching. Ruddock and McIntyre (2007) believe that listening to the learners can lead to significant changes in teachers' perceptions of their students, and this can lead to a greater readiness by teachers to be open to change and to even enabling them to gain renewed excitement about their teaching. Arnot and Reay (2007) also say that listening and responding to what students may say about how they feel or react as learners can lead to teachers examining and often improving their own practice. The overall argument here is that more meaningful discussions about learning which emerge through a response to student voice can lead to school improvement (Mitra, 2009; Rhodes and Brundrett, 2010).

The importance of student voice being valid

Despite all the potential benefits of student voice noted above, these are unlikely to occur unless the student voice and its use are completely genuine. It is necessary to note therefore, some of the warnings and reservations that relate to this. If the voice is controlled by teachers or leaders and is not a genuine reflection of what students are saying, then it is not likely to be effective. This point relates to the extent to whether 'student' voice is speaking for all students, and if for some, for which ones? The concept of a 'voice' can obviously disguise a very complex constituency, such as a student body, as Fielding (2007) warns.

Further, if the voice of the students is limited to commenting on the 'service' they receive, then, although that in itself has some value, it is reducing the students to consumers or customers and Arnot and Reay (2007) suggest this may in effect be legitimizing the marketization of education. As Gunter and Thomson (2007: 27) argue, if the learners 'are positioned as traders rather than citizens, then their voice as learners may be silenced or at best be hoarse'.

If either of the parties involved, that is, teachers and students, feel that the process smacks of tokenism or manipulation, clearly only lip service will be paid to the concept. If, for example, teachers believe that student voice is merely to improve measurable learning outcomes for enhanced school or college status, it will soon become something that teachers and lecturers are 'required' to do and this desirability on the part of leaders and managers 'slides smilingly into compulsion' in the words of Fielding (2006: 307). Compliance and control quickly become the context within which this initiative may be set! Bragg's research (2007) noted that some teachers felt that student voice could be a threat to their professional identity and purpose, a point we shall return to later.

On the student side, if the learners PERCEIVE that the student voice is being used for adult purposes, then they will not be willing to develop the concept and it is possible that it may make things worse and they will feel 'used and abused' (Fielding, 2006: 306). Rather than enhancing relationships, there is a risk of cynicism and disenchantment on the students' part, with very little chance of mutual respect developing.

School councils have often been the first step in initiating student voice in many schools and colleges and indeed, they are now compulsory in many countries. At best, they can offer students valid opportunities to contribute to school decision-making, but this is not always so. For example, research by Burnitt and Gunter (2013) into primary school councils in England found significant limitations, both in terms of adult personnel and more importantly in terms of areas of decisions. They found very little evidence of leaders utilizing their councils for anything linked to strategic matters and concluded that there was an argument that the councils were likely to be seen as a 'pseudo-democracy' (2013: 61). Whitty and Wisby (2007) were clear that unless student voice initiatives were linked primarily with learning, then they were likely to stay at the level of 'chips and lockers' (2007: 2). This is not to deny that the use of school lockers, for example, is not very important to a 11-year-old, because it can be – and anxiety about security of personal property could certainly affect peace of mind and consequently effective learning. This however, should be essentially a starting point only.

Learning of course is not confined to the classroom, and there are strong examples of students of various ages being effectively involved in recruitment and selection processes (see Parker, 2011 and Kent, 2012). Whatever its use, we need to state that we believe that there are three main ways in which student voice can be used highly effectively:

- that it is primarily focused upon learning,
- that it is based on operating in a way that is genuine, incisive and as professional as possible,
- and it is done as part of a partnership with teachers.

We refer to the use of student research within a school or college and we now focus on that.

Student research

For teachers to improve in their practice, they need effective feedback, and this needs more than the immediate response of 'That was great' or 'A bit boring, wasn't it?' While other teachers and lecturers, leaders, mentors, tutors can all play invaluable roles in giving feedback, students are the most likely to notice issues in teacher practice because they are observing their teachers day in and day out – in fact they are in a unique position. They are also most likely to notice changes in practice when they occur. If the feedback from students is based on a carefully constructed, mutually agreed investigation into practice, then the value to both teacher and learner can be very significant.

The starting point is the question as to what is to be investigated. Who initiates the process by identifying the topic for investigation? It may be the individual teacher or lecturer and the process would then ideally follow as shown in Figure 3.1.

Alternatively, an issue may be identified at a subject or departmental level, for example following some kind of review, audit or inspection. In this case, the process is similar and as shown in Figure 3.2.

Two actual examples will help to illustrate this. Case Example 3A shows how an individual teacher who felt she needed help encouraged her class to

1. Teacher identifies an issue
2. Teacher/learner discuss and agree focus
3. Method(s) agreed
4. Research carried out
5. Data analysed *together*
6. Report agreed
7. CPD needs identified if appropriate
8. CPD provided
9. Teacher modifies practice
10. Evaluate and revisit after agreed period.

    (Steps 7 and 8 may not be needed.)

FIGURE 3.1 *Individual teaching focus.*

1. Subject area or school identifies an issue
2. Issue discussed and agreed with teacher
3. Learners consulted and focus agreed
4. Method(s) agreed between teacher(s) and learners
5. Research carried out
6. Data analysed by learners
7. Report written and agreed with teachers
8. Report to subject area or school
9. Action agreed (may include CPD)
10. Teacher modifies practice
11. Evaluate and revisit after agreed period.

FIGURE 3.2 *Subject area focus.*

identify what she needed to do to improve an aspect of her practice. Case Example 3B describes how a subject department used student research to investigate an area for improvement identified by a leadership review of its practice.

CASE EXAMPLE 3A

NEVER TOO YOUNG!

Donna was a teacher in her third year with a class of 7-year-olds. As a good teacher, she became aware that her questioning in class always seemed to get responses from the same six to eight children and it was almost impossible to get many of the others to answer. Her knowledge of child development meant she was aware that at six or seven, children are becoming very aware of their peer group and felt she could set the children an investigation.

A group of four children (two who were voluble, two who were very quiet) devised entirely by themselves a simple questionnaire for *all* the pupils, asking them why they might not answer a question in class and so on. A series of statements using the happy/unhappy face scale was used:

Donna found that she was surprised at just how afraid many pupils were of appearing silly in front of peers, or of not being able to express themselves in answering. She says, 'I completely changed my approach by, firstly, asking very few open questions to the whole class, but instead selecting individuals and then praising them for trying to answer however incorrectly. It all sounds so simple, but I also feel I now know *all* of my children better and I am fostering a philosophy that it is alright to get it wrong or to say you don't know. I believe the class learning is now much more effective and relevant!'

CASE EXAMPLE 3B

CATCHING THE EYE

An internal leadership audit of the Science Faculty in a college situated in Dublin had led to a report which included criticism of the learning environment as 'lacking in stimulation and appearing largely irrelevant to the students' learning needs, especially current ones'. Tim and Martin, two students, were commissioned to research what was needed. They used questionnaires, with stratified sampling, interviews with staff and observations, which included watching people's attitudes as they passed a display.

'We also would stop people in a corridor or coming out of a lesson, and ask them whether they had noticed a display or poster, or whether a teacher had indicated something to them in class. We then posted various posters and other 'visuals' in rooms and classes, and repeated the exercise.'

Conclusions? Tim and Martin found that displays in classrooms made no difference at all unless a teacher used them or drew attention to them while teaching.

They also found that the one eye-catching place for 'visuals' was on the stairs, especially facing people in stairwells. Such displays there could then be used to direct attention to displays elsewhere.

The Faculty's policy has completely changed and the teaching 'using the visual "teaching environments"' is now one of the criteria used in lesson observations in the college.

Research development? Tim and Martin confess: 'We should have had a female in our research team – they do have a different perspective!'

These two examples are not the only way in which a piece of student research can be initiated of course. In a school or college, or an individual classroom, where the learners are sufficiently emotionally mature, and perhaps in a culture which has developed to encourage this, the learners themselves may identify an issue for investigation. The process would be as shown in Figure 3.3.

1. Learners identify issues
2. Learners/teachers discuss and agree focus
3. Method(s) agreed
4. Research carried out
5. Date analysed *together*
6. Report agreed
7. CPD needs identified if appropriate
8. CPD provided
9. Teacher modifies practice
10. Evaluate and revisit after agreed period.

FIGURE 3.3 *Learner focus.*

The culture may need to be a particularly supportive one because of the need to avoid a teacher feeling vulnerable or even threatened if students themselves suggest an area for improvement, especially in the teaching/learning process. However, in the following case example (Case Example 3C), the focus was on organization in the learning context, which was less likely to be thought threatening to teaching practice at the stage the school was then at in terms of its research-based development.

CASE EXAMPLE 3C

In terms of the students carrying out the research, it is absolutely crucial that they apply the same rigour to their processes as any other researchers do, professionals or practitioners. The key principles stated in Chapter Two can be restated here, that is, that the research should:

- be honest and use an ethical approach throughout,
- have a clear purpose,
- recognize its limitations,
- use the right instruments for the right purpose,
- come to any conclusions based on actual evidence,
- make recommendations for action if possible, and
- enable the researcher(s) to learn from the process and do even better next time.

It really is important that such principles are as rigorous as for adults. Any attempt to 'water down' the approach is not only insulting to the young people and children concerned but will render the research findings much less valid and therefore much less useful. Kellett (2005: 1) usefully describes researching with children as researchers as being able 'to distil rather than dilute' the process.

However, children and young people are not actually adults and some differences are inevitable. Skills in, for example, data analysis will be at a lesser level and the writing of reports may be in a more immature expression. These skills can be learned and will develop. The area of ethics in research perhaps needs greater clarification and emphasis with children and young people when researching in a school or college because of the very nature of the relationships that exist there. Ultimately, the adults there are in a position of authority and responsibility. Indeed, in most countries they are, by law, 'in loco parentis' and in the last resort responsible for the child's or young person's actions. It follows therefore that when, for example, a pupil is interviewing a teacher, it is not the same as one teacher interviewing another teacher. There are lines which may not be crossed and some protocols which need to be followed. The protocols of confidentiality and privacy are obvious to a teacher carrying out practitioner research because their professionalism includes a commitment to child protection from harm. Students carrying out research in their own school or college therefore, need to be completely clear that everything they learn through their research about the views and perceptions of adults is bound by a commitment to complete confidentiality, unless specific permission is given otherwise. Indeed, they should be told that the same data protection laws apply to them as to anyone else. One could add that in these days of instant comment via social media in which today's youngsters grow up, this is an invaluable lesson to learn. The authors of this book have found in running sessions for secondary students about ethics in research, that some of the most searching questions they have ever faced emerged. Here are two to digest:

> If you are interviewing a teacher and you are sworn to confidentiality, and the teacher tells you something about his past that is clearly inappropriate for a teacher, what should you do?

> If another student tells you something very personal about herself during an interview, and you believe she needs help, but she has told you in complete confidence, should you report it?

Perhaps your thoughts on these can help you to be ready for when students engage in debate about research ethics with you!

Unless such ethical issues and procedures are strongly stressed, the balance in relationships between teachers and learners can be upset and this can be hard to recover from, especially if problems occur in the early stages of establishing student research.

Linking with professional learning and CPD

As already discussed in this book, professional learning is much more than formally organized courses. It is bound up with concepts of lifelong learning, and with teachers' notions of themselves on a personal as well as professional level. We have suggested how a professional learning community may be developed using collaboration and reflection and enhanced by using practitioner research into practice. Student research adds another dimension to this. In addition to the benefits for the effective teacher of encouraging self-reflection, constant questioning about practice and sharing ideas with colleagues, it:

- Gives the teacher or lecturer the learner's perspective.
- Offers the learner the chance to see the teacher's perspective.
- In a subject area, for example, it can offer implications for all teachers working in that area and enable collaboration for learning.

1. Teacher(s) and learner(s) identify issues *together*
2. Discuss and agree research focus
3. Agee method(s)
4. Carry out research
5. Data analysed *together*
6. Report and action agreed together
7. CPD needs identified (if relevant)
8. CPD provided (if relevant)
9. Teacher modifies practice
10. Evaluation and revisit after agreed period.

FIGURE 3.4 *Partnership focus.*

- Can foster much greater understanding of relevance in what is being learned and how it is being learned. In this lies a key benefit in that this is helping future citizens become less docile in accepting what they are given. Instead, they may be able to work more independently, ask the right questions and, when they challenge, do so on the basis of well-constructed enquiry, not just because it does not fit in with personal likes or dislikes.

- Can develop teacher/learner relationships significantly and encourage more dialogue about learning, so that it becomes less of a concept of 'your learning' and more of one about 'our learning', surely one of the most important steps forward that can be taken. In this respect, we would see the ideal model of student research following the 'partnership basis' procedure, as shown in Figure 3.4.

Two case examples can illustrate the way in which teachers' CPD and professional learning can be developed through student research. In Case Example 3D the research outcome was an organized CPD programme. In Case Example 3E, the outcome was some 'soul-searching' and development of a mid-career teacher.

CASE EXAMPLE 3D

ASK THE LEARNERS!

Claire was a Geography teacher in a recently established academy in a large city in the East Midlands of England. She became very concerned about the homework of her class of Year 10 (15-year-olds and in a pre-examination floor), both in terms of its content, presentation and irregularity of handing in the completed tasks. She faced the class over this and the students confessed, defensively claiming it was 'boring', 'not worth doing' and 'didn't count in the exam'. Claire decided to hand the problem to them and they accepted the task of investigating the situation.

A group of four students were selected entirely by the class and included one who assiduously completed homework on time and one who very rarely even completed. A questionnaire to all class members and a rigorous interview with Claire herself about the purpose of homework led to findings which suggested that many of the problems lay in the nature of the task being set.

Fortunately for Claire, she found a course being offered to all the academies across her chain and attended, coming away with 'a wealth of ideas, and a completely new approach to setting "out of class" tasks as we now called them'. Claire's belief was that 'not only were the research findings and my CPD follow-up invaluable, but I am certain that the sheer fact that the students took ownership of the issues through research meant that, from then on, "we" were doing this, not me just doing it to them'.

CASE EXAMPLE 3E

NEVER TOO OLD EITHER!

Gary was a teacher approaching fifty years of age; he was a history teacher in a secondary school in a relatively prosperous area of Southwest England. He was at the top of the salary scale, his lessons all good and his exam results were regularly well above average, both for his school and nationally. With a decade to go before any retirement prospects, Gary had become aware that he was not getting as enthusiastic responses from his students as formerly. Eventually, he confessed this to a class of 15-year-olds, and was amazed and 'flattered' by their understanding. After the initial banter ('Your jokes are getting worse, sir!'), the students decided to investigate the issue for him.

With his permission, a group of four students devised a survey across all Gary's classes for 14, 15 and 16-year-olds. The questionnaire used was quite open, as it was headed 'Helping Mr X!' The questions asked what the learners liked and did not like about Gary's classes, and what they felt would help them to (a) enjoy them more and (b) learn more from them. The findings were collated, summarized and given to

Gary with the group's own recommendations (the group had shared the findings with their own class to make these proposals).

When Gary received these he was 'so devastated, so that I hardly slept for three nights'. Why? 'It was clear that overall I was perceived as nice but bland, even boring, efficient (I got them through their exams) but not stimulating. Worst of all, it was clear to me that they felt there was no deep learning going on – just stuff to get them through tests.'

'Eventually, I took a good look at myself as a teacher and as a person – it was time!' I had slipped into a comfortable and unchallenging routine. It seems odd but the first thing I did was change my holidays! My wife and I did something different in the summer – backpacking in Chile instead of guest house in Norfolk. That helped the thinking no end! My lessons for next term were prepared in a totally different way.

'My class's reaction next term when the topic was "Aren't you fed up hearing about wars all the time?" instead of "Reasons for World War One" was surprise, to say the least. One of my biggest changes was when my students now ask me whether I know something is often to say "No I don't. Why would I? I'm just one person. What about you?"'

To many people, this may sound simple, but Gary's teaching and students' learning is much more effective and much more enjoyable for both parties. Equally important, his final decade in the profession and his life overall he reports as being 'so much more interesting and I know my retirement will be too!'

Possible barriers to implementing student research

The potential opposition to encouraging students to get involved with in-house research may come from four possible sources: the teachers, the students themselves, the leaders and occasionally the external stakeholders, such as parents.

- Opposition from teachers is likely to rest in reservations teachers may have about letting their students or pupils examine aspects of their work. Some will feel that their professional status is threatened and some that their actual authority will be undermined. By revealing what they feel may be perceived as 'weaknesses' or 'inadequacies', they may worry that some learners will exploit these 'flaws'. They will therefore be reluctant to give these learners opportunities to scrutinize them closely, as they see it, and as one teacher expressed it to one of the authors who had pointed out it could lead to improved teaching and learning, 'Yes, but they might say I only improved with their help!' It took some time for that teacher to realize that that statement was a positive, not a negative one!

- Reservations from students or pupils often come from the belief that such initiatives are only going to be available to certain learners, meaning the more able and articulate ones. In some cases, this view springs from experience of poorly managed student voice, such as school councils where only 'pseudo democracy' operates, as mentioned earlier. Other reservations may relate to the amount of time needed to be invested and, particularly for students in important stages of school or college life when examinations are near, they feel it may be a distraction from the pressure to perform, however limited the teaching might be.

- Reservations of school or college leaders usually are based on a misunderstanding of the point of genuine student voice, a personally held philosophy about the authority status of staff and leaders being jeopardized, or one which believes that the adult/child relationship balance in society is to be maintained in traditional ways. Another possible reason is that such an initiative will be unpopular with parents and the community and the institution's reputation will suffer as a result.

- This is the other area where reservations may exist. Particularly in schools where pupils attend for the statutory age period, parents may query why pupils are helping professionals to improve –'Surely that is what professionals do for themselves, isn't it? They go on courses and so on. I don't go to my doctor and expect to tell him how to do a better job.' This is one comment reported to the authors as a school contemplated initiating student research.

How can these reservations be overcome? For leaders and managers who are committed to student voice and student research, the above reservations need to be acknowledged and tackled head on.

The first simple way is simply by showing how effective it is. A belief in learners' involvement in their own learning leading to the kind of effective processes already described is the best possible answer. The second is about communicating to all those with the reservations. The best communicators when any scheme is up and running are the students and pupils themselves of course, telling parents and governors about their own research and the developments that have ensued after research.

Initiating and developing student research

In the final part of this chapter, it might be useful for those considering it to suggest some of the ways in which schools and colleges have initiated the process of student research and then gone on to develop it. Drawing on their experience, the following may be considered by those who feel that the initial response to the suggestion might be lukewarm:

- Find the right students! Advertise for school researchers, stressing that the job is open to anyone and go through some kind of relatively gentle recruitment and selection process (it may become more rigorous later!) Explain what it can involve, the ethics and above all the purposes of the process – better for them, the teachers, the school. In that order. Invite teachers to be present at the initial recruitment meeting. Ensure that in the final selection, a range of students is chosen, gender, ethnicity, and ability for example. Suggest that they work in small research teams, perhaps about four people per group.

- Tell the students – and mean it – that the results of their research WILL be recognized and acted upon where appropriate. Where they are not acted upon, reasons will be clearly given to them. Tell them about the plans for presenting and disseminating the results and build status into this, for example by getting them to report formally to a leadership team.

- Choose non-threatening topics initially such as those that focus on physical environment, physical resources, services, school organization or policies. Stress that these all affect learning and teaching however, and this is the reason they need researching.

- Encourage simple research instruments such as surveys via a questionnaire initially. Quantitative surveys on how popular a certain change has been or a proposed one can be valuable and are relatively easy to administer and analyse.

- As far as staff are concerned, get the keen ones on board at the start. Arguments to encourage others less keen include assuring them that their professionalism is not under threat – they are the qualified, experienced, mature experts. Tell them the truth which is that one of the benefits of student research has been shown to be that learners discover just how hard teaching is and how much work goes into even a single lesson (Parker, 2011), thus increasing respect for the teachers.

- Where necessary, inform governors and parents of the process explaining the process. Perhaps suggest students reporting to a governors' sub-group or parents' group at some point.

At all points, stress that the focus is on improvement – in student learning, in teaching and of course overall school or college improvement. There is evidence that student research can lead to improved attendance, behaviour and exam attainment (Watkins, 2001; McGregor, 2004)

Summary of Chapter Three

This chapter has:

- described the growing importance of student voice,

- considered the benefits and purposes of student voice,

- explained why the voice needs to be valid,

- suggested ways in which student research can be valuable and effective,

- considered some barriers to introducing student research and strategies for addressing these and

- suggested ways in which student research might be introduced and developed.

CHAPTER FOUR

Improving professional learning at whole school level

Introduction

In the previous two chapters we have considered the strategies required to develop the professional learning potential of individual staff and how best to develop a school or college in which in-house inquiry becomes a natural part of the institution's life. In this chapter we look at how such individual or small group approaches can be related to the whole school or college and incorporated into development planning and corporate strategy. Increasingly schools and colleges are being encouraged to work together either as part of a chain, network or federation and we will look at how this interdependence and cooperation can be fostered. This chapter therefore:

- describes the importance of the development of a 'learning organization',

- considers how schools and colleges are working in partnership and networks,

- identifies how professional learning contributes to the development of effective planning and strategic development,

- discusses the importance of monitoring and evaluation to sustain continuous improvement,

- establishes the need to identify clear dissemination procedures to facilitate the sharing of research findings and

- stresses the importance of appropriate professional practice and the establishment of a strict set of ethical guidelines.

Developing a 'learning organization'

There has been a wide range of terminology used to describe what we will refer to as a 'learning organization', for example: the healthy organization (Miles, 1965); organizational learning (Argyris and Schon, 1978, 1995); communities of practice (Wenger, 1998) and learning organizations (Senge, 1990). It is reasonable to assume that by definition a school or college should be a 'learning organization'. However, many who have worked in schools and colleges would testify that this is often not the case and in some instances, an anti-learning culture can prevail. According to Bell and Bolam (2010: 102) learning organizations 'are predicated on a broad view of education, shared learning, wide-ranging continued professional development and the involvement of all stakeholders in the educative process'. This enhanced view of professionalism evident in a 'learning organization' should enable all stakeholders (students, teachers, parents and senior leadership) to work closely together to bring about continued classroom improvement and lead to a raising of standards. The characteristics of a 'learning organization' have been summarized by Bush and Middlewood (2013: 225) who suggest that they:

- focus their energies and activities on learning, recognizing that learning may come in many different forms as appropriate to a wide range of learners;

- establish and develop an ethos and ethic of enquiry;

- recognize that learning can come from many sources – not just from formal teaching; external networks and stakeholders such as parents also contribute to learning;

- accept that learning is a lifelong process and that the organization's role is in making a contribution to this process; and

- are in a continuous transformational state.

This is quite a daunting list and it suggests that a school or college that succeeds in becoming a 'learning organization' will be a stimulating place to work or study and there will be a great deal of activity and development. Any school or college that achieves this state will, according to Parker and Middlewood (2013: 130), see the development of 'a culture of positive restlessness'. This culture should involve all members of the school or college community and it is important to recognize that everyone has a contribution to make. This should be valued and celebrated by the school or college and teachers, support staff, catering, cleaning, technicians and students all have a valuable contribution to make. However, without a proper structure and effective support mechanisms 'a culture of restlessness' can quickly deteriorate into chaos. It is essential that procedures be put in place, that enable creative thinking and action to take place within a structured and safe environment. Teachers and lecturers are used to dealing with change, often externally driven, and the opportunity to initiate their own change should be welcomed. However, it is important to distinguish between purposeful change and change for the sake of it. McCharen et al. (2011: 689) have identified that a 'sense of shared purpose is a notable aspect of a learning organisation'. This can go a long way to convincing staff that they should embrace a 'culture of positive restlessness' as a key factor in the creation of a learning organization.

If the school or college can get this shared purpose to develop into a purposeful change model that can work it can have a beneficial impact on the overall performance of a school or college. A number of authors have commented on the importance of the development of 'learning organisations' as a significant factor in bringing about school improvement; see, for example: Muijs and Harris (2006) and Stoll et al. (2006). Liljenberg (2014: 4) has identified five key aspects that are significant in identifying a school as a learning organization:

- Organizational structures
- Goals, visions and values
- Responsibility and decision-making
- Reflection and evaluation
- Attitudes.

CASE EXAMPLE 4A

A SALUTARY LESSON

A large urban primary school situated in an area of high deprivation had an extremely proactive and positive senior leadership team, supported by the Chair of the School Governors, who fostered the development of a learning organization within the school. Despite the school being in an area of high deprivation, jobs there were always highly sought after, and there was no issue with recruitment or retention of staff. A whole range of support mechanisms were put in place to ensure that all staff and students were involved in developing and maintaining the 'learning organization'. Staff were encouraged to be proactive and to take risks despite the pressures of a rigid National Curriculum and the continual pressure of maintaining an Ofsted-rated 'outstanding school'. Staff and students had created a 'learning organization' where:

- learning was at the heart of all aspects of school life;

- the school had a positive culture where risk-taking and experimentation was encouraged;
- students were enabled and encouraged to take part in research and development;
- all staff were entitled to a structured programme of staff development opportunities ranging from short programmes to a school-based MA;
- Research-led teaching was encouraged;
- there was involvement with a wide range of external organizations and a genuine sense of collaborative working;
- all staff felt that they had an equal role to play in making learning effective;
- sharing was encouraged;
- there was a high degree of involvement with new initiatives.

These five factors have to come together to create the right conditions for the creation of a 'learning organization'. Once established that it is an ongoing process to develop and remain as a learning organization and it is important that particular procedures are acknowledged within the school and college to ensure that the five aspects are underpinned by the factors identified by Bell and Bolam (2010). Having achieved the status of a 'learning organization' there will be an ongoing requirement to maintain momentum as the environment and circumstances change over time. As we pointed out earlier in the chapter, the momentum has to be maintained by the generation of new ideas and fresh approaches. There will be a need to undertake continuous review and development to sustain a learning organization. There is a sense that once the right conditions are established this process can continue indefinitely. However, as we show in Case Example 2A, a school where we have worked on a number of enquiry and professional learning programmes, this is not always the case.

This had taken several years to achieve and the school and the headteacher had a positive local and national reputation. There were always large numbers of partners eager to work with the school, the staff and students. In 2011 the Chair of Governors decided to retire from her post and as a consequence in 2012 the headteacher decided to follow suit and take early retirement. An external candidate was appointed as the new headteacher and the deputy head, following her failure to get the headteacher post, applied for and was appointed as the headteacher at another primary school.

The new headteacher did not share the same enthusiasm, as her predecessor, for the maintenance of a 'learning organization' and quickly dismantled many of the systems and structures that had been put in place. Experimentation and innovation were replaced by conformity and an emphasis on hierarchy and managerialism. The culture of the school changed markedly and a number of staff decided to leave the school and recruitment of replacement staff became difficult. By 2014 the school had lost its Ofsted 'outstanding' rating and had become a school that was in relative decline. In two years the 'positive restlessness' had been replaced by negative apathy.

Working in partnership

In the next chapter we will consider in detail a range of collaborative professional learning approaches within and across institutions. However, here it is important to report that over the last two decades there has been significant pressure on schools and colleges in England, for example, to work more closely together and to involve the wider community in this process. This is despite the counter pressure being applied by other government policies for schools and colleges to compete for students and resources and the establishment of a quasi-market in education (Abbott et al., 2013a). There have been numerous attempts to encourage schools and colleges to work together through loose federations and the establishment of consortium arrangements. There has been a long tradition of schools and colleges working with higher education institutions on areas such as teacher training, staff development, accredited programmes and research initiatives. There is also a long tradition in many schools and colleges of working with other external organizations such as employers, private sector training organizations and charities.

Recent developments including the establishment of teaching schools have encouraged schools and colleges to take greater responsibility for the initial training and continuing professional development of teachers and other members of staff. Teaching schools are expected to raise standards as part of a self-improving and sustainable school system (DfE, 2010). They have been given a key role to play in the leadership of a self-improving education system. Working with a range of partners, including other schools, Universities, academy chains and the private sector, teaching schools are expected to establish alliances with other organizations to raise standards and to improve the overall quality of teaching and learning. There are a range of roles that teaching schools are expected to undertake including: initial teacher training, continuing professional development and leadership development, school-to-school support and a specific focus on developing research within the classroom across the wider school and in collaboration with other organizations (NCTL, 2014).

The development of academy schools as part of a larger academy chain has also provided significant opportunities for groups of schools to work in partnership over a range of issues including professional learning and research (Salokangas and Chapman, 2014). Organizations such as universities, independent schools and further education colleges have been encouraged to set up and manage primary and secondary academy schools. Several high-profile independent schools have set up primary and secondary academy schools. Universities have opened their own schools or set up university teaching schools. A proliferation of partnerships across different sectors has been encouraged by the coalition government in England.

Despite all these developments there are still some opportunities for schools and colleges to work in partnership as part of a local-authority–led initiative (Abbott et al., 2012; Smith and Abbott, 2014). Historically the local authority had a significant role to play in encouraging schools to work together, provide development opportunities for staff and to disseminate good practice. As the powers of the local authority have been diminished, by successive governments, increasingly the main role of the local authority is to act as an 'honest broker' and promote effective conditions for schools and colleges to work in partnership.

Clearly, working in partnership with other organizations, especially partner schools and colleges, has a number of potential advantages:

- Operating across a number of organizations provides the opportunity to draw on a wider range of expertise and experience.

- Organizations are able to share knowledge.

- Partnership provides a structure to disseminate good practice to enhance professional learning.

- Support can be provided from 'stronger' organizations to those who require support.

- Greater access can be provided to a wider range of financial, physical and human resources.

- Joint planning and development can take place.

- Increased cooperation should lead to a reduction in duplication and the wasteful use of scarce resources.

- It will be possible to disseminate good practice over a larger number of organizations.

- New relationships can be encouraged and fostered.

It is important to acknowledge that any attempt to promote increased partnership working between organizations also has potential pitfalls. Leadership and ownership are two obvious examples where conflict might arise. The use and allocation of resources is also another potential area for disagreement. It is important that clear ground rules are initially agreed and accepted by all those involved in the partnership. Ideally these ground rules would be arrived at through negotiation and consent. However, new models of organization often do imply hierarchical arrangements with 'lead' or 'managing' schools or colleges being given the authority to direct events and perhaps, more importantly, resources. (The 'Beacon School' initiative in England was a clear example of such models.) Whatever system is in operation, it is reasonable to assume that there will be some agreement about sharing ideas, ownership, evaluation and ethical considerations. Failure to clarify these issues at the outset may lead to serious problems later on as the partnership becomes increasingly complex. We will return to consider some of these issues in more detail later in this chapter.

Effective planning and strategic development

Developing a whole school or college approach to professional learning should lead to enhanced performance and to improved outcomes for students. Over the previous thirty years there has been a significant emphasis placed on the role of effective planning and strategic development in schools and colleges (Abbott et al., 1991). According to Hargreaves and Hopkins (1991: 91) the main objective of strategic development planning is 'to improve the quality of teaching and learning through successful management of innovation and change'. Planning for strategic development is now embedded into the culture of schools and colleges and activities associated with the development of the professional learning of the school or college staff should be incorporated into these plans. Given the competition for scarce resources it is essential that a school or college develops clear strategies and identifies priorities to ensure efficient and effective use of resources. Parker and Middlewood (2013: 130) advocate the notion of the 'big idea' to make sure 'that each year is seen as a new challenge to introduce something which is innovative, which is school-wide and which captures the imagination of most if not all the staff'. Development plans are usually set over a three-to-five-year time period, but are reviewed on an annual basis and this would provide the opportunity to introduce the 'big idea'. In relation to professional learning it is expected that the planning process should include elements of the following:

- Identification of the core aims of the school and how these relate to the development of professional learning and the establishment of a learning organization.
- A clear statement about the purpose of the professional learning activities envisaged during the lifetime of the plan.
- A commitment to professional learning for all staff and ways in which students will be involved in the process.
- Details of the actual activities and projects that will take place with a justification why these have been identified as priorities.
- Allocation of sufficient resources to particular projects.

- Identification of the staff who will have responsibility for the project and those that are likely to be involved in the professional learning.

- Establishment of a clear timeline with identification of monitoring points.

- Clear targets which establish measurable outcomes.

- A detailed system of evaluation and monitoring that can contribute to an ongoing systematic review of activities.

CASE EXAMPLE 4B

A 'BUZZING' SCHOOL

As a routine part of the planning process, within a large comprehensive school situated in the northeast of England, professional learning and enquiry projects are included as one of the key components. All staff are encouraged to put forward suggestions for projects that can last from a few weeks up to three years. A systematic review process is put into place with clear outcomes being identified. As the headteacher put it in an interview for this book:

'We do get some wonderful ideas being put forward, and also some that might appear to be a little strange. It can be time consuming but it's worth it when you see the reaction of staff and students. It's important that we value everything and are able to justify why we might say yes and no. What we're keen to do is to foster a spirit of enterprise, enthusiasm and enquiry. Even if it appears crazy it's always welcomed and given due consideration. You have to keep the creative energy going.'

Examples of some of the ideas that have been developed include:

- Introduction of a programme of mindfulness for students and staff. This has, according to the school, contributed to a reduction in stress levels.
- The employment of former students to act as learning mentors. This has had a beneficial impact on the current students and also provided opportunities for mentors to gain valuable work experience.
- Introduction of Mandarin as an additional subject. This has proved very successful, but the demand has exceeded the capacity to deliver the subject at the right level.
- Developing links with the local primary schools by allowing them greater access to some of the specialist facilities at the secondary school. The primary schools welcomed this, but the pressure on space has forced the school to impose strict limitations on this initiative.

These are interesting examples, but the key is the way in which they are incorporated into the planning process. As a science teacher at the school commented:

'It's great because you know if you've got an idea, it'll be listened to and if it's any good it'll be given a chance.'

If the development plan is going to be successfully implemented, it is essential that all staff are consulted and feel some degree of ownership and involvement. If the plan is imposed, or is only seen as a statement created by the principal or senior management, then it will be extremely difficult to develop projects that have any chance of a successful outcome. In many schools and colleges one member of staff will be given the responsibility for leading professional learning and this person should act as an advocate for the development of professional learning. This post is a key role in any school or college and the postholder should play an active part in the planning process acting as a conduit between staff and senior leadership. Failure to listen to staff or poor implementation of plans can quickly lead to apathy and staff will rapidly disengage with the process if they feel only lip service is being paid to the development of professional learning. Therefore it is important that any plans are realistic and achievable. That is not to say that everything has to be successful and in many cases valuable lessons can be learnt from initiatives that fail. However, it is important that a proper evaluation and monitoring system is put in place. Failure to have an effective evaluation monitoring and reporting system is likely to lead to a lack of focus and a potential waste of resources.

Monitoring and evaluation

Given the amount and pace of change which will occur as a consequence of becoming a 'learning organization' it is important that a school or college devotes sufficient time and resource to the development of an effective monitoring and evaluation system. It is essential that significant emphasis is placed on monitoring and evaluation but in a large number of cases unfortunately this is not the case. Too often schools and colleges find themselves consumed in a continuous cycle of activity that prevents proper reflection and analysis. This is further exacerbated by the amount of policy change directed at schools in various countries by central government policymakers, and there is a danger of initiative or policy overload as one initiative is quickly followed by another. As Faadhilla, a vice principal with responsibility for staff development at a further education college in the East Midlands, said in an interview for this book:

> No sooner do we undertake professional learning with staff for one Government initiative then we have another and another. We never seem to have time for any sort of evaluation. As a result we cannot systematically tell you what works and what doesn't. It's difficult to motivate some staff because they have the attitude that it doesn't really matter because the next thing will just come along. I really wish we had time to properly monitor and evaluate what works and what doesn't.

Monitoring, according to Walker (2010: 188) is 'the power of watching and feeding-back'. In practice this means that participants involved in some aspect of professional learning or enquiry and those managing the process actually know what is happening within a particular project. This sounds an easy and obvious process, but in a busy school or college with a range of different professional learning activities it is easy to see how difficult this can be in practice. It is essential, therefore to establish clear monitoring procedures that are transparent, time-constrained and consistent. This will then give staff and students confidence in the system and they will be able to see that due value is given to the available evidence. Once information is collected it will then be possible to provide feedback to those involved in the process. This should occur on a regular basis to enable any necessary changes to be made. Monitoring will enable effective decisions to be made and play a significant part in ensuring that effective professional learning takes place.

Evaluation is a continuation of the monitoring process and involves making some judgements about the effectiveness or otherwise of particular initiatives. Just as monitoring should be governed by a particular process, the same applies to evaluation. Again, this has to be an open process involving a range of participants, although an effective decision-making process has to be in place. The data gathered from the monitoring process feeds into the final evaluation of any particular project. A decision can then be made, either to continue, change or stop a particular project. Communication and involvement are key aspects of this process. It is important that participants are involved in the process and their views are taken into account. Once the available evidence has been considered it is important that any decision is clearly communicated and justified. There have to be fixed points in the process, but in a learning organization the process of evaluation followed by clear decision-making should be part of a continual effort to bring about positive change.

Clear objectives at the start of the entire process will make the final evaluation much easier to complete. Having clear objectives to measure the findings against to see if the objectives have been achieved will enable clear decisions to be made about the effectiveness of a particular initiative to foster professional learning and development. At the outset it is worth devoting sufficient time to the creation of clear objectives, because it will make the monitoring and evaluation process so much easier to complete. It is too easy to get carried away with a particular project without identifying systematic and measurable objectives. Time not devoted to this activity will result in difficulties later on and may, in the long run, make it more difficult to justify continuing or expanding the project.

Monitoring and evaluation have to be part of an ongoing cycle of improvement. This should be a systematic process with clarity regarding the decision-making process. Creating an organizational culture where there are many opportunities for professional learning is what schools and colleges should be striving for, but this has to be supported by effective structures and systems. Failure to develop these structures and systems at the outset will cause problems later on and lead to disillusionment with any process of professional learning.

Dissemination

As we mentioned in Chapter Two, dissemination will depend on the institutional context and recommendations. There is obvious merit in any project that leads to improvements in the quality of teaching and learning in one classroom, but there is so much more benefit if the factors that contributed to that development can be disseminated to a wider audience. Again, this seems a perfectly reasonable and obvious point to make but we are sure that many readers will be able to recount cases where no effective, or in some cases, any dissemination has taken place following the end of a particular project or initiative. Staff and students can all too easily get carried away in the planning, development and actual doing of any particular professional learning or research project. We recognize this from our own work with serving teachers and lecturers who often carry out very valuable pieces of research on classroom practice or school organization for an MA thesis, but it subsequently is only seen by their examiners. The teachers and lecturers either lack the confidence to share their work with others or, more commonly, there are no procedures to disseminate their findings. This is all the more surprising when often their school or college has made a significant financial contribution to their studies. In our own work, at a university, we have to be careful not to take the attitude that 'once the research is done we can move on to the next project'. Dissemination has to be an integral part of our work. For busy staff in schools and colleges this is an even greater problem. Their focus is on students and their own classroom and there is a danger that any dissemination of findings is not done properly.

It is important that a dissemination process is incorporated at the outset into any professional learning or enquiry project. This process should set out clear guidelines and a timetable for the dissemination to take place. Staff and students who are involved can then develop a proper dissemination plan and there will be a clear expectation that some form of dissemination will take place. A structured dissemination will add value to the work that has been completed and will enable participants to receive acknowledgement of and feedback on their work. The structure of the dissemination should also be agreed in advance and be carried out in a supportive and non-threatening environment.

The type of dissemination can take a number of forms and will depend on culture, practice and the relevance and applicability of any outcomes. Decisions relating to the type of dissemination should, of course, be based on a common school or college approach. However, it is reasonable to assume that opportunities to participate in the dissemination process will normally be extended to the whole school or college. Just because a particular piece of professional learning or enquiry has taken place in the English department there should not be an expectation that it remains within that particular department. There may well be lessons for the whole school or college from the work carried out in the English department and staff and students in the English department may benefit from the feedback given by colleagues from other subject areas. However, there may be occasions when it is perfectly valid to restrict the dissemination to a limited audience. To be successful a particular professional learning or enquiry project does not have to have applicability to other areas, but it is important that other areas are aware of what is happening. Whatever option for dissemination is chosen it is important that it conforms to the agreed conventions for dissemination across the school or college.

The purpose of the dissemination process should be to contribute to improvements in the quality of teaching and learning in the school or college. If a 'learning organization' has been established there will be ongoing staff development activities and the dissemination procedures can take a number of forms, including:

- Written materials including a regular bulletin
- Case studies
- Presentations
- Use of social media
- Workshops and training events
- Publication in professional or academic journals.

Some schools and colleges, and especially academy chains, have gone a step further and have started to commercially produce materials based on professional learning or enquiry projects carried out in the institutions that are part of their group. While this should not be the starting point, or driving force, for any particular project it does provide the opportunity for widespread dissemination to take place.

CASE EXAMPLE 4C

PERSONAL AND INSTITUTIONAL DEVELOPMENT

Anna, a lecturer and programme manager at a large further education (i.e. post-compulsory education) college, had significant vocational experience and qualifications. She had not undertaken any significant academic study, but as part of a college-wide professional development programme she was encouraged to study for an MA in Educational Leadership. Following the successful completion of her MA programme Anna was enthused and decided to go on to study part time for a professional doctorate (EdD). Her study initially focused on distributed leadership within the college. However, in her work as a programme manager issues relating to teaching and learning became significant to her and also across the wider college. As a consequence Anna decided to put the two together and look at distributed leadership in relation to teaching and learning. She gathered data from all levels within the college and she realized that there was a significant lack of effective communication and an absence of an appropriate policy that was able to improve teaching and learning. Recognizing the significance of her work, the college encouraged her to address these issues and to disseminate what she had found out. As a consequence she began a structured dissemination programme, including disseminating her findings in a variety of ways:

- Presentation to all staff in the college
- The provision of staff training as part of the staff development programme
- Presentation to college governors
- Presentation and provision of training to senior managers on how to facilitate distributed leadership
- Development of a new teaching and learning strategy for the college based on her enquiry project.
- Externally she presented at staff development conferences and made significant use of social media,
- Given the level of external interest in her work she was able to publish in professional journals.

What started as a small-scale study for a post-graduate qualification developed into a project that had major implications for the college as a whole. In particular, through the dissemination process, teaching staff started to realize the role they had to play in the leadership of learning within and outside the classroom, workshop or laboratory. Following the culmination of her Ed D programme, Anna was appointed as the teaching and learning coordinator at her college.

Ethics

We are surrounded by debates on ethics and issues such as confidentiality, misrepresentation and cheating. Too often, there can be negative connotations. However, any school or college committed to developing professional learning through enquiry projects needs to have an overt policy on how this will be subject to ethical considerations. In this way, a whole school or college approach can be developed. These considerations should be clearly laid out, agreed on by participants and consistently applied. These are discussed in detail in Chapter Two.

Each school or college needs to have its own ethical policy and, for example, there may be specific requirements relating to student participation in projects, rules about making contact with parents or guidance relating to the dissemination of findings. However, any policy will also have to take account of the wide-ranging national legislation in the relevant country that governs ethical issues; these are likely to include laws about data protection and various ones that deal with equalities issues such as in gender, ethnicity and age. Such individual organizational policies need to be in place before any enquiry takes place. Written procedures are required and documentation may be required to ensure consistency and importantly to protect the organization and any individuals against potential accusations (there is often an ethical approval form that has to be completed before the commencement of any project). Higher education institutions have an ethics committee to consider ethical issues relating to research and enquiry projects. While not advocating this level of bureaucracy for every school and college, there is a clear need to ensure consistency of approach. Middlewood and Abbott (2012: 78–9) have identified five key terms to ensure implementation of appropriate ethical safeguards:

- *Confidentiality:* At the start of any enquiry guarantees are given to participants about the confidential nature of the enquiry and there should be agreement about the ways in which data can be used.

- *Anonymity:* There will be clear agreement that participants have the right to remain anonymous and that any data about individuals will be treated sensitively and not identify individuals.

- *Privacy:* Confidentiality and anonymity give a guarantee of privacy for the individual. However, privacy should also extend into the informal area and there should not be 'off the record' conversations or communication about individuals or groups.

- *Sensitivity:* There is a need to be sensitive to the demands you might place on individuals or groups as you undertake the enquiry. The person conducting the enquiry also needs to keep a 'distance' to ensure objectivity.

- *Honesty:* It is best to be open about issues and to openly discuss what has been said or what has been found out. This may well involve some form of compromise, but honesty as part of the enquiry process is really the best policy!

One of the major ethical issues facing staff in schools or colleges is the dilemma about advantaging one group over another. If an intervention is introduced to improve the quality of teaching and learning, in for example, Year 7 history, should this be undertaken with the whole year group or just one group? If the intervention is confined to only one group, then that group could potentially benefit or lose out in comparison to the rest of the year group. Equally, the introduction of an untried approach with the whole year group could disadvantage all Year 7 students who study history. This is an ethical dilemma that can only be resolved by those on the ground operating in their particular context. There should be ethical procedures in place and these must be consistently applied, but the final decision about the form that any intervention in the way in which Year 7 history is taught, remains with those involved and affected by the project. The participants in the project should be able to justify whatever decision is made and clearly communicate this to all those who are involved. At the core of the ethical debate should be appropriate professional practice and those involved have to take ownership of this increasingly, often contentious, and important area.

Summary of Chapter Four

This chapter has:

- described the importance of developing a 'learning organization',
- considered how schools and colleges and other organizations work in partnership,

- identified the role that professional learning and enquiry play in the development of effective planning and school development,

- discussed the importance of monitoring and evaluation,

- established the need to identify and develop effective dissemination practices and

- considered the issues relating to the development of appropriate professional practice and the introduction of ethical guidelines.

CHAPTER FIVE

Collaborative and team approaches to professional learning

Introduction

In Chapters Two and Three, we proposed principles for carrying out effective practitioner research to enhance the professional learning of individual staff, and suggested ways of involving students or pupils in this. Now, having considered in Chapter Four the importance of a whole school or whole college approach to professional learning, we examine the potential for identifying the learning needs of teams and link this with possible collaborative approaches to in-house research. This chapter therefore:

- describes some of the practicalities of effective practitioner research,

- considers how to avoid research overload,

- discusses the potential for team approaches to identifying learning professional needs, and proposes ways in which these can be effectively practised,

- describes how collaborative professional learning can be encouraged and developed,

- stresses the importance of ensuring that everyone has the opportunity to be involved and

- discusses collaborative learning across institutions.

The practicalities of effective practitioner research

In carrying out an in-house inquiry, whether as an individual, with one colleague or in a group, the first requirement is that it shall be of high quality, genuinely and professionally operated. The principles already described in Chapter Two need to be applied and every precaution taken to observe professional courtesies. For example, if an investigation into the underachievement of male students in modern languages is to be researched, permission should clearly be gained from the Head of Languages. In fact, in one post-statutory college in the West Midlands of England, written permission of this kind has to be obtained and then shown to any affected person each time a stage of the research is carried out.

Rigour must be applied to each of the methods used in carrying out the research which usually means prior training is involved. Any kind of superficiality is totally unacceptable. A good example here is of Learning Walks. This is a method which is not really used by professional researchers but has become a valuable tool in practitioner in-house investigations. As noted regularly, informal learning is hugely important and therefore relaxed or incidental observations, informal and unplanned discussions, and walks around the school or college are all crucial parts of a culture where learning is occurring and should be seen as normal. However, they should NOT be confused with structured observations, interviews or learning walks! These informal and valuable aspects are important but cannot be used as a basis for proper assessments of or judgements on practice or performance. A Learning Walk is a structured process, a specific 'Learning Journey' (Middlewood and Piper-Gale, 2011: 37). 'The focus of the walk is carefully chosen and questions formulated before the walk takes place. The focus must be adhered to 'avoiding publicly stated comparisons or anecdotes – and most, importantly, being judgemental' (ibid.: 38). As with other research methods, only when the data on the chosen focus has been collected and analysed should any conclusions be drawn.

Other fundamental procedures need to be adhered to in all inquiry processes. Middlewood and Abbott (2012: 171) proposed a set of 'golden rules' for researchers and included, as relevant here:

- 'Ensure you know which data you need to collect before deciding upon the method of collecting the data.
- In sampling, decide first on which people and then on how many.
- Ensure you keep the presentation of your data separate from your analysis of the data.'

Such procedures help to ensure that the outcomes of the in-house inquiry that uses them will have validity and thereby in many cases generalizability to some other situations and contexts.

This book is a good deal concerned with the use of in-house research to lead to improved professional learning and CPD because the precise focus for the learning can be identified through a rigorous investigation. However, it is vitally important to understand that the process of carrying out such an in-house inquiry is in itself a significant form of professional learning. Richard Parker recognizes this and notes its impact in the case study described in Chapter Seven. We note here some aspects of that learning (not in any specific order):

- Clearly, some of the specific skills involved in carrying out research are learned – such as devising questionnaires for surveys, constructing schedules for observations, analysis of documents, creating time logs or diaries. When one reflects on how many separate occasions observations will be used in educational institutions, to take but one example, it is clear that such skills will not be wasted.

- Participants learn to base their views about professional matters – and probably others as well – on evidence rather than make assumptions.

- They learn not to assume that the obvious 'answer' is not always the right one and that because something was true previously, it does not automatically that it is true forever. Herr and Anderson (2008) describe how a US school's staff were convinced that the poor test scores in the school were the fault of the students who missed the most classes. However, the data from the attendance figures and test scores showed that was very little correlation, with some regular attendees scoring poorly; this forced the teachers to examine their own teaching more closely to find the reasons.

- They learn that usually one set of evidence or data may not be sufficient and triangulation is needed by getting evidence from at least one other source. This can simply be another point of view. Interestingly, two quite separate examples in later chapters show that if the viewpoint of primary pupils or secondary students had been sought with regard to the colour of the learning environment, instead of just those of the designers/architects, a more effective learning stimulus could have been in place much earlier!

- As far as learning in groups is concerned, participants learn about sharing ideas, open-mindedness, interdependence, power sharing as well as gaining in individual and collective confidence.

Of course, many of the above are life 'lessons' which can sound trite, but educationalists at all levels are first and foremost individual human beings and often such 'lessons' have to be experienced in a professional learning context for them to acquire meaning there.

Avoiding research overload

In a research-engaged school or college, which was discussed in Chapter Two, there may be a risk especially before the desired culture is fully established that some staff will feel they are being 'hounded' by too many requests to become involved in research. We have heard the groan of 'Oh no, not another questionnaire!' being uttered in more than one institution! However enthusiastic the person proposing the research is, and however willing people are to help, there will be occasions when that enthusiasm and willingness will be sorely tested. Since it is essential that all participation in in-house research is entirely voluntary, it is important to bear in mind this factor, and plan the whole approach with the possibility of people becoming jaded in mind.

What are the considerations to be noted?

First, an overload of anything is not really welcome! If so many people are investigating practice and procedure at the same time, at least three consequences are likely:

1   People will only feel their workload is being added to and schools and colleges are already very busy and often stressful places anyway.
2   There could be such an excess of data and findings accumulated that no one will have time to read all the ensuing reports and some will inevitably be ignored or abandoned.
3   People may become disenchanted and the desired culture will not develop.

Second, we need to remember the purpose of the practitioner research in the first place – to improve practice where needed and to do this through enhanced CPD and professional learning. The research is not an end in itself. Although this sounds obvious, remembering the investigation is a means to that end needs constantly to be stressed. Indeed, if an excess of research occurs, can any programme of CPD/professional learning cope? For an individual to improve in practice, one step at a time would seem to be appropriate. Therefore, in putting forward a request for help with research, the emphasis should first be on the area to be investigated and how the help can be given as second.

Third, there clearly needs to be an overall strategy and plan for implementation for professional learning and CPD, as discussed in the previous chapter. Such a plan will involve timing, with a schedule for carrying out a programme over a specified period. Of course, plans are never set in stone and situations may occur when something has to be delayed or brought forward, but overall priorities will be clear and the research and consequent programmes can be managed effectively. An external inspection, for example, might highlight unexpectedly an area of concern in a specific area of practice and the school or college leaders feel that this needs to be investigated earlier than had been planned.

Fourth, not only does there need to be this overall strategy and plan in terms of areas of practice in general, but it is essential that detailed records are kept of every single piece of practitioner research, indicating for example where the research was done, how many people were involved, what kind of research methods were used. Of course, because of the anonymity of the in-house investigation respondents, the actual identity of participants is not recorded, but consulting the records would quickly show, for example, which subject areas, which staff in particular roles had been involved and need to be avoided for a period perhaps; similarly for pupils and students.

While much of this is being described in negative terms, it is of course good practice that such records are used positively, for example in finding out when a particular issue was last addressed, whether the person concerned has now left the staff and other such matters. In this way, the records become a valuable record of school/college improvement and a tool for future improvement.

Collaborative approaches to in-house research

We mentioned in Chapter Three that many students, perhaps most, in beginning in-house research prefer to work in small groups or teams. This is because as beginners, it is easier and reassuring to work with others and learn together as the work takes place. Above all, working in a team gives confidence to a novice and in many cases where students are concerned; they may prefer to continue to carry out their inquiries in this way. Of course, this way of working can be just as useful for anyone beginning the activity for the same reason. We know of support staff in schools or colleges who have strongly preferred to start like this, and sometimes teachers, although if they are carrying out the work for an accredited programme, they need to ensure that they seek permission first from the appropriate higher education authority. Universities, if they permit collaborative research for a course, insist on it being possible to be clear on submission of work that specific parts are attributable to individual members of a group.

Of course, teams for in-house inquiry can equally be of mixed role composition, such as a blend of teachers, administrative and support staff. Indeed, there are some topics which are best tackled by such a mixed team, especially when a working relationship is being investigated. It is worth noting what can be the benefits of using a team approach to some in-house research:

- As noted, it can give greater confidence to the people concerned, especially if one or more of those involved is beginning research for the first time.

- Obviously, the workload can be shared – very important for busy people!

- The scope for the investigation can be much greater or wider if several researchers are involved.

- Therefore a larger amount of data can be gathered.

- If the team is carefully chosen, a greater range of research skills can be used, with the burden not falling on just the one person. Thus, people who are comfortable with quantitative research and 'number crunching' can link with those more at ease with qualitative data. Those who are good at interviews can link with those who prefer surveys and there are also writing skills and data analysis skills to be utilized. One considerable benefit here is that members of the research team can develop specific skills other than those which are perhaps more natural to them by working with each other. It is sound advice to beginners to 'play to your personal strengths' initially and then develop others as you progress. This learning can be formally structured if required. For example, someone nervous about carrying out an interview with someone senior in the institution can perhaps act as an observer at an interview carried out by the person who is happy to do it. (This must be with the permission of the interviewee of course, with the normal ethic 'rules' applying.)

However, for a team approach to in-house inquiry (or indeed any form of team research) to be effective, it is essential that a strongly consistent approach by all team members be followed. For this to happen, we suggest that:

- A rigorous debate occurs about the methods and the sampling to be used and agreement is then reached in which everyone understands why those methods and samples have been chosen and that it is essential that everyone then follows the same procedures in applying them in the same way.

- A similar debate should occur about who does what in terms of dealing with respondents. Who should interview whom? Should friendships be irrelevant? Is it appropriate for gender or ethnic issues to be taken into consideration? As long as these are all aired openly and honestly, then all members will be clear about the consistent approach to be taken when agreement has been reached.

- A similar debate should underline the strict ethical guidelines that will be followed by all team members in carrying out the investigation. There will probably be context-specific issues here that must be agreed, for example, how interviewees will be addressed by name. Simple though this sounds, even trivial, one interviewer addressing an interviewee in a much more familiar manner than the others can cause problems in terms of responses elicited.

- We would recommend that the agreed 'rules' are written up and recorded and all team members have copies for their regular reference.

Collaborative professional learning and CPD

As shared learning is an important feature of effective schools and colleges which should be encouraged, specific plans to enable this to happen should be in place. These involve 'support between at least two colleagues on a sustained basis', (Cordingley et al., 2004: 2). While shared learning in an informal sense remains a vital part of an organization's learning culture (e.g. chatting with colleagues about a particular child, class or strategy), we are here concerned with more formalized collaboration. Some research (Kasl et al., 1997) has indicated that the very nature of team work is in itself a significant learning experience for all team members. However, because teaching is inherently an individual practice, we need to note carefully any prerequisites for effective collaborative professional learning.

- Sufficient time being available. This is both easy to state and often difficult to achieve, but without the time, the sharing may remain at a superficial level, the worst example of which is simply some people copying from others what they see as good practice. While some initial benefit can accrue from this, only with the intense scrutiny and debate involved in 'real' sharing can lasting changes be achieved.

- Willingness to share. The sharing needs to be primarily voluntary, rather than forced or contrived, so that the sharing is a genuine two-way process and so that trust becomes a crucial ingredient in the whole process. If the collaboration is managed via a top-down approach, there is a risk of the 'contrived collegiality' (Hargreaves, 1994) resulting, with the possibility of a long-term negative impact.

- Enthusiasm of those participating. King (2011) found that enthusiastic people taking part in a collaborative learning project in the Republic of Ireland strongly influenced others, including some who had previously been unwilling to be involved. Given the time, willingness and enthusiasm, King found that the ensuing changes in practice showed 'evidence of deep learning which is a prerequisite for sustaining practices' (ibid.: 152).

- Recognition of the individuality of each learner. While each individual in a team will equally have scope for learning, it is important that each person be seen as an individual learner with their own learning needs. This may depend on age, stage of career, experience, as well as perhaps capability and ambition. In other words, while teams may work as groups in learning, each single person has the right to be treated as the unique individual that they are. Although people are different, they should have equality of status as a learner. Slater (2004) suggested that it was crucial that people were seen as of equal status so that the input from any individual was equally valued, whatever its ultimate contribution to the final outcome.

- Awareness of different favoured learning styles of people. One obvious recognition of differences between people is that people often have preferred learning styles through which they learn most effectively. In collaborative or team approaches to professional learning, where different team members for example have different preferred learning styles, this needs to be acknowledged. Where the learning is to occur in a semi-formal context, then it is clearly helpful if people have had the opportunities to find out which is the style most appropriate to them, using diagnostic tools. Such tools include visual, auditory, kinaesthetic (VAK) testing, emotional quotient (EQ) testing, a brain hemisphere diagnosis or a neuro-linguistic programming analysis. Of course, where a school or college has attained the stage where it sees itself as a professional learning community (as in Chapter Two), then such analyses will be the norm, enabling appropriate delivery for example of more formal learning. These styles are not rigid of course and learners often develop several effective ones, but in an initial team approach, it is important that these differences are recognized, to avoid some learners being unintentionally neglected.

What are some of the benefits of shared professional learning?

- There is a greater likelihood of consistency of effective practice emerging. Morris and Hiebert (2011) argued that only through jointly developed teaching practices could teaching be continuously improved, and while many would not go as far as this, there is no doubt that students and pupils benefit from a consistent approach and attitude to teaching and learning in their specific school or college context. Consistency in no way of course means uniformity!

- The learning is context-specific. If leaders for example are comprehensively aware of the local context, and thus can analyse the needs, attitudes and strengths of colleagues, the ensuing learning can be the most relevant and effective for all those concerned (Zhang and Brundrett, 2011). Collaborative learning means that all those involved share the same knowledge of the same clients and stakeholders and can therefore focus more coherently on their specific learning needs.

- By its very nature, shared learning is challenging. It is more challenging than individual learning because the internalization which occurs in individual learning has to be externalized for others to share and critique as appropriate. Some people will deal with this more confidently than others, at least initially. When staff do debate learning processes and then challenge each other's views of them, the end result will almost certainly be that overall a deeper kind of learning will emerge. These processes, likely to include trial and error, reflection, experimentation and others, lead to participants gaining confidence into how these fit their own developmental needs and which are adaptable in their own practice.

Approaches to shared or team professional learning

Where in-house inquiries have led to a specific issue being identified as one for improvement in practice across several related practitioners, such as those in a subject department, it makes sense for a team approach to professional learning or CPD to be considered. If, for example, a classroom issue such as quality of teacher questioning, use of group work, effectiveness of teacher feedback, needs addressing, the teachers concerned would undertake shared professional learning or CPD. This might be relatively formalized CPD with an 'expert' on the topic leading the development sessions, or it might be organized internally with those involved committed to their own development. In either case, given that all those have the same role (in this case classroom teachers) the following questions could be the starting point:

- WHAT are we trying to improve?

- WHY are we trying to improve it? (This may seem very obvious but we believe it is possibly the most important question. Who is the improvement for? How will it help them? To achieve what? These sub-questions are the start of the debate about professional learning, its purpose and professionalism as such.)

- What common goals are we aiming for?

- What scope for individuality exists within our common proposal? (Or must we all do the same?)

- How will we evaluate the effectiveness of our new practice?

Where the learning involves people with different roles (e.g. teachers and teaching assistants), the first three questions above would be the same and then:

- What specific focus is there for us – as teaching assistants (TAs)? As Teachers?

- What aspects of the relationship (between Teachers/TAs) will need adjusting in the light of the changes?

- How will we evaluate – together and separately – the effectiveness of our new practice?

In this mixed role learning, it is crucial that each role holder understands the implications of any practice change for those in other roles. An obvious method to adopt here is in the form of role play or role-swapping, where the teacher becomes the assistant for a while, and vice versa, really getting to grips with the reality of any change's impact and not just seeing it from their own perspective.

In their research into the development of extended schools with a community emphasis, Middlewood and Parker (2009) found several examples of teams of people with a large range of roles to serve the diverse clients. Many of these adopted a team approach to most of their professional practices including their review and appraisal and their training and development. One such team used the following approach (adapted):

Given the focus for development has been identified, for example, the need to improve our one-to-one sessions with individual students, through a survey of students, the first thing is for each of the team members to write down how they approach and manage these sessions. They do not identify pluses or minuses, it is simply descriptive.

Step Two. Each person swaps the papers on which this is written. This surprises some people but we see it as crucial. We cannot defend our approach because it is not ours! When you hear your own work read out by someone else, it is sometimes humbling and you can more readily notice any weaknesses that way. While listening to each one, including your own, you make notes on them – carefully putting two columns of www ('what works well'), and ebi ('even better if').

Step Three. We clarify any queries-whether anyone feels misrepresented (they only have themselves to blame as they wrote it!).

Step Four. Together we list on a chart all the www's and discuss at length – so that what should emerge is the amalgam of the very best parts of current practice that we shall not want to lose in any changes we propose.

Step Five. Then we list all the ebi's and here the focus is on change! The self-criticism is fierce and we often need to go back to the first list to remind ourselves how much good already exists!

Step Six. Finally we agree what changes we will try to implement in our practice. We note any reservations that individuals have and record them, noting that person X will be able to alter something because of specific circumstances.

Step Seven. We do a final summary list – very important – of how we feel the students will gain from the changes.

Step Eight. We agree dates for implementation and for meeting to review the new practice, asking people to keep notes at the time they occur of any issues that arise.

One of the strengths of this kind of approach is that everyone has the chance to learn from someone else; there are no 'stars', and everyone feels supported. The new learning that has occurred has been developed from current practice, especially the 'best bits' of it, and the debate that took place enabled challenges and diversity of views to be addressed. Individuals have a chance to learn of effective practice without their own being denigrated and are more likely to be positive about the proposed change.

A by-product from successful collaborative professional learning is often that new relationships are formed and developed and that these can sometimes then be used in other areas of the school or college practice. For example, where two or three colleagues have found they have enjoyed working and learning together, they will have discovered each other's ways of working, how to complement each other's skills, and how to learn from each other. Given that, they may well volunteer to work together in another aspect of the institution's development, or be asked to do so by a leader who has seen how effective they have been. Case Example 5A is a good illustration of this happening.

CASE EXAMPLE 5A

RECOVERING FROM A FALSE START

A large Sixth Form College (providing for 16–19-year-olds) in the South East of England has also a significant number of adult education classes, in the daytime and evening. Janet was Adult Education Co-Ordinator and studying part time for a Masters' degree in Business. For the HRM Module, she wanted to investigate whether the development interests of associate staff were better managed through the curriculum areas to which they were attached or by forming a separate department for all personnel in the college, who were not teachers. Attempting to collect data in a survey questionnaire, she was surprised at the apathy, opposition and even hostility, she received. 'People felt they would be seen as disloyal and also maybe it was personal!' said Janet.

She had done plenty of reading on the topic but was giving up the survey, when a small number of staff approached her and the group (a science technician, a language assistant, the Librarian and a subject HoD) set about the inquiry because of their interest.

A series of workshops and seminars followed, with each of them dealing with a presentation on:

My job: what I do.

- What I like and what and don't like about it.
- How do I develop in the job and learn to improve.
- How my learning needs are met.

Gradually other staff – teaching, clerical, technical and support – asked to join ('if only to tell others how important their job was!' said most) until more than twenty were attending and raising all kinds of questions. ('We learned so much about each other, the college and about learning itself.') Interestingly, questions arising were less about the functional aspect of roles, but about motivation and job satisfaction. This led to others undertaking reading on these topics and reporting back.

Eventually, a report was produced for the perusal of the college leadership – not an official one, as the whole thing was voluntary. When the leadership team offered to organize the workshops, the offer was refused! ('We felt it would alter the dynamics for it to be official.') However, a number of issues in the report were effectively addressed and the seminars continue. Presenters include staff from all parts of the college and on a relationship level, Janet said, 'People I'd never spoken to previously are now good friends and some of them are following accredited courses together as well.'

Ironically, the original issue of subject area or separate department has actually never been resolved, but as Janet said, 'It probably doesn't matter as our learning needs are being met now anyway – by us!'

Opportunities for everyone

In the conventional teaching school and colleges of the twentieth century, there was for the most part, a clear assumption that only teachers and lecturers could be involved in investigating their own professional practice and following up with any appropriate training or development. Other employees in the institution were there to support these key staff, whether directly (such as assistants and technicians) or indirectly (such as administrative and premises staff). However, the roles of such personnel and their part played in the overall learning of students and pupils have been significantly developed and, in developed countries primarily, their importance has been increasingly acknowledged (Emira, 2011; Bush and Middlewood, 2013; Graves, 2013).

In an inclusive culture to support learning across a school or college, the contribution of everyone will be recognized and therefore the professional learning and training and CPD of every single person is important. If any group of people is neglected, this will signal that learning is only relevant to particular employees and ultimately that the members of that group can continue doing things in the way they have always done, regardless of the constantly changing environment within which school or college exists. It therefore is crucial that when opportunities for improving personal learning are offered, no one should feel excluded. In any case, in an institution where everyone recognizes that it is a focus on learning which binds them all together, all work is ultimately seen as a contribution to the key purpose of learning, whether the daily work involves cleaning the building, providing meals, maintaining equipment or keeping records, work which can sometimes – superficially – be seen as more remote from student learning. It follows that all people should not only have access to the opportunity for relevant professional learning and development, but also to investigate what changes might be needed in work practice and how to address these most effectively. In Chapter Seven, in an extended case study, the principal of a large community college describes how this inclusive culture was striven for as a matter of principle and attained through insistence on the right of everyone to be involved.

Those working in schools or colleges with children or young persons with special learning needs often provide some of the best examples of collaborative learning. Brian, a deputy head and Acting Head at an all-through special school in the Milton Keynes area of England, said in an interview for this book, that:

> If you go into most of our classrooms and see several adults involved with the pupils there, you would usually find it impossible to tell which were teachers and which were other staff, such as assistants or carers. They are all working – and learning – together for the benefit of the pupils.

In such a case, as far as professional learning is concerned, Brian's statement that everyone has expertise which deserves support and the development of that is crucial. 'There is no hierarchy of knowledge here,' he said, 'so what an assistant brings back from a structured programme, an in-house seminar, or a specific inquiry is as valued as the detailed expertise that a teacher might bring back from attending a Masters course.' Case Example 5B (below) is based on such an inclusive approach.

CASE EXAMPLE 5B

NO ONE ALWAYS KNOWS BEST!

The special school for children with learning difficulties of various kinds, physical, emotional, behavioural and mental, became concerned that the activities and general atmosphere at morning break and lunchtimes was unsatisfactory and sometimes having a negative effect on subsequent lesson behaviour and attitude. After the issue was identified at a general staff meeting, a group of six assistants and lunchtime supervisors volunteered to 'look into it'. They decided to carry out observations of the current situation first and devised observation sheets, which they checked for usefulness with a teacher doing a Masters at that time.

Over two weeks, behaviour was carefully noted, both quantitatively (through tick boxes for numbers of incidents, for example) and qualitatively (through personal notes made).

With the observation data collected, the task of analysis began, which turned into a much bigger one than anticipated. When variables such as the weather, location, facilities, staff on duty and so on, were considered, some patterns were discernible. Jean, the senior teacher with overall responsibility for behaviour, helped and eventually the patterns were agreed. 'Easy solutions were not an option', the teacher sad, 'because whilst one proposal might solve this part, the problem would simply appear to move somewhere else'. It was then decided to interview a sample of both pupils and staff, to discern their perceptions of the data and seek proposals. The pupil focus groups were all led by assistants or supervisors, and the staff groups by teachers.

The feedback from the pupil focus groups showed pupils' clear recognition of the situations as described by the data, whereas the staff groups – especially the teachers in them – shared much greater surprise at the data. 'It appeared that the assistants, supervisors and pupils were more aware than the teachers of what was going on' said Jean. 'We only tended to focus on the aftermath.'

The resultant proposals included:

- Some new equipment for specific use of more physically able pupils (to avoid over-usage on facilities for the least physically able);
- Specific training provided for two of the assistants;
- A change in break times;
- An amendment of staff duty rotas.

The situation was regularly monitored and formally reviewed after a year from the original observation. It was found to be significantly improved.

Collaborative professional learning across institutions

By the final decade of the twentieth century, it was becoming virtually impossible for schools – and for many post-statutory colleges as well – to be effective as isolated institutions. Fullan (1998: 2) described the change as the walls round the schools as 'tumbling down metaphorically speaking – as government policy, parent and community demands, corporate interests and ubiquitous technology have all scaled the walls of the school'. In many developed countries, policymakers, leaders and others saw the dangers and impracticalities of schools operating in comparative isolation. Many factors contributed to this outlook and included:

- A realization that education alone was not a panacea for all societal problems and an integrated approach was essential.

- Research showed the huge number of influences on learning in a life and formal schooling was only one, albeit very important.

- Pressure on public services, including education, especially via pluralist, multi-ethnic societies.

- Realization that the huge sums of money expended on those at disadvantage were not paying dividends and there was a need to move from remedial to preventative approaches.

- The lack of coordination and cooperation between various public services became increasingly clear, exposing a lack of clear accountability when problems occurred.

All these meant that communities were better served by institutions working together for common causes and in the case of education, institutions working together to provide a more effective service to all those in a community. The initiatives of Every Child Matters (England and Wales) and No Child Left Behind (United States) were overt attempts to address some of these issues. While political will altered with different administrations, the impetus and requirement for schools in particular to work together remained, and indeed was supported by various formal structures for collaboration, even in the basically competitive or quasi-market markets that exist.

Sometimes, collaborative professional learning emerged naturally from various partnerships or federations. For example, Abbott et al. (2014) found that researching school-to-school partnerships in a large urban area, most schools in an effective partnership had developed joint CPD or some form of learning without it being an original part of the official plan. Furthermore, this joint learning was above all found to be effective when it was 'mutual learning' with each school staff learning from the other, even though the structure of the partnership was based on one 'successful' school supporting another. This mutual learning is perhaps the key to effective cross-organizational collaboration. In England, various partnership structures which the national governments have established – and provided funding for – have involved the idea of a 'good' supporting a weaker or a leader among a group of schools (e.g. the 'Leading Edge' groupings). Research such as that of Arnold (2006), Connolly and James (2006), Rutherford and Jackson (2008), has indicated that such notions encourage initial resentment in some cases, and that the collaboration flourishes with the recognition that everyone has something to learn from someone else. Leadership by a school or college in such cases is therefore best limited to one school or college being the main administrator or facilitator of the group. Perhaps some resentment is inevitable in a competitive environment, because of the conflict between collaboration and competition (Stevenson 2007).

In cross-organizational learning therefore, the professionalism of teachers and other educationalists involved is shown to be key in that it is this that develops the necessary mutual learning. In arguing that an 'absence of dependency' was essential for successful collaboration, Arnold (2006) was simply stressing what lies at the heart of professional learning per se, that everyone has something to learn and to offer and returns us once more to the notion that the best teachers are also highly effective learners. Where the staff of two or more institutions therefore collaborate, the potential for this is considerable – subject to good organization of course. The scope for informal learning in such a context is also of course considerable. Case Example 5C describes a situation where collaboration across schools outside of the normal transition arrangements was established and unforeseen learning as well as the planned outcomes occurred. Four schools (two First Schools for 4–9-year-olds, a Middle School for 9–13 and an Upper School for 13–18) liaised annually as the pupils moved from one school to the next, but the schools felt they could learn much more from each other than the usual curriculum coordination.

CASE EXAMPLE 5C

EVERYONE GOOD AT SOMETHING

The four schools in a city in the north of England believed there was much more they could learn from each other than merely what stage in the subject curriculum pupils had reached. Trevor, PD coordinator at the Middle School, explained that, 'We wanted to avoid any hierarchy to remind ourselves that we are all dealing with the same children, only at different ages. It sounds obvious, but often children felt as if they were starting all over again each time they moved schools.'

A programme of collaborative development was agreed and each school was asked to state:

'What are we really good at?'

It was agreed that these topics would be chosen not by the school leaders but by a survey via questionnaire to all staff (subjects were not allowed to be mentioned!)

One of the primary schools chose parental involvement and the other support for special needs pupils as their very best strengths, the middle schools chose assessment for learning and the upper school use of technology.

A programme of visits, teacher exchanges and workshops in schools run by staff from other schools was arranged. 'There was huge scepticism from some teachers', commented Trevor, 'especially over the suitability of practice for one age group being applicable to another. We heard comments about parents of children that age not being the same and so on. It was of course, about learning the principles behind the specific practices and then about adapting them to practice in the new context. It was a tremendous success, not only in the structured programme but also in the relationships that developed across the schools. Secondary staff were particularly impressed by the primary approaches they adapted.'

The evaluation showed that not only in specific outcomes, for example Upper School attendance at parents' evenings increased by 20 per cent, but in other areas, such as:

- Respect and admiration for the work done by teachers of different age children grew enormously.
- Realization that traits, in child development could be tracked through the child's school career.
- Understanding that some professional learning was common to all staff, regardless of the ages of the children they taught.

Furthermore, Trevor added, 'Our actual transition arrangement improved through our understanding of the children and staff.'

Summary of Chapter Five

This chapter has:

- described some of the practicalities of effective practitioner research,
- considered how to avoid research overload in a school or college,

- discussed how a collaborative approach to in-house inquiry can work,
- discussed the principles and practice of shared professional learning,
- briefly noted the need to ensure inclusion of everyone in these practices and
- considered the issues involved in collaboration across different institutions.

CHAPTER SIX

Improving professional learning at individual classroom level

Introduction

It is a common criticism in many school and college staffrooms that professional learning and especially educational research is too far removed from the realities of the classroom. While we were undertaking the research for this book, a comment by a deputy headteacher of a large primary school summed up the prevailing mood:

> Professional learning has to be relevant to the classroom, otherwise it can be a pleasant activity but it'll be viewed as a waste of time. As for educational research, it's so inaccessible and even though I know many teachers who would love to be involved, you academics do a good job of putting them off. Relate it to what we do in the classroom and involve classroom practitioners and we might get somewhere.

Teachers and lecturers are extremely busy and work in a pressurized environment and it is essential that professional learning and inquiry does relate to their work. There is a distinction to be made between teachers and lecturers who make use of research evidence and those who actually carry out the research in their own classrooms or organization. Judkins et al. (2014: 13) report on a classroom teacher who claimed that 'since we have embarked on our own research project . . . we have thought about and looked more into educational research and theory to support the research that we are carrying out'. There is likely to be a connection between making better use of external research and practitioners developing school- or college-based research projects. In Chapter Two we considered the issues associated with the development of a research-based school or college and the opportunities to establish effective practitioner research that can lead to the development of a research-based professional learning community. In Chapter Three we looked at the need to involve learners in inquiry projects and in particular the growing importance of student voice. In this chapter we focus on the drive to increase the use of research in schools and colleges and the development of the skills required to carry out classroom based inquiry. In particular, this chapter:

- stresses the role of professional learning and enquiry in the development of improved classroom practice and student attainment,

- proposes the development of models of good practice that focus on the classroom,

- discusses the principles of effective classroom inquiry,

- describes ways of using research evidence in the classroom,

- outlines the principles of action research and

- describes in detail ways of developing practitioner research in the classroom.

The role of professional learning and inquiry

As we point out in Chapter Two the major focus of a school or college is learning. It is vital therefore that professional learning and inquiry has a direct correlation to the classroom where there can be the biggest impact on learning. We will start, in this chapter, to consider what is possible and the current state of debate surrounding the role teachers and lecturers should play in their own professional development and how this can feed into improving classroom practice and learning. There is an increasing focus on building evidence into education. Goldacre (2013: 7) has argued that teachers and lecturers should take responsibility for developing their own classroom practice:

> Firstly, evidence based practice isn't about telling teachers what to do: in fact quite the opposite. This is about empowering teachers, and setting a profession free from governments, ministers and civil servants who are often overly keen on sending out edicts, insisting that their new idea is the best in town. Nobody in government would tell a doctor what to prescribe, but we all expect doctors to be able to make informed decisions about which treatment is best, using the best currently available evidence. I think teachers could one day be in the same position.

Developing evidence-based practice as part of a drive for school improvement has been part of an ongoing debate. Hargreaves, in his 1996 Teacher Training Agency annual lecture, argued that greater use should be made of research and evidence (Hargreaves, 2007). He was also critical of the quality of a significant amount of educational research and this was supported by the Hillage et al. (1998) and the Tooley and Darby (1998) reports which were also critical of the quality and content of much educational research. Internationally, a number of studies have highlighted the need to develop an evidence-led approach designed to foster continuing school improvement; see, for example: Hargreaves and Fink (2006), Lambert (2007) and Lowsted et al. (2007). There has been a growing consensus that working together, the development of a professional culture and allowing teachers to take greater ownership and responsibility for what happens in the classroom, can lead to significant school improvement (Fullan, 2001; Hargreaves and Fullan, 2012). As we show in Chapter Four increased school autonomy should enable schools and colleges to take greater responsibility to bring about changes in practice. School-based research according to James (2104: 34) enables fundamental questions to be asked of teachers and lecturers: 'How do we know what we are teaching is actually having a beneficial effect on our students? Where is the evidence? And, if there is evidence, how transferable and testable is the intervention?' Teachers and lecturers have always wrestled with these questions, but there is a strong movement within education to develop a system that is based on evidence rather than just experience or fashion.

Durbin and Nelson (2014: 2) argue for evidence-informed practice which they describe as 'research evidence collected through systematic and established formal processes, normally by professional researchers'. In practice this can be difficult to achieve in an organized and systematic manner, given the fragmented nature of a great deal of educational research. To overcome this Durbin and Nelson (2014: 3) advocate that:

- School-level needs and interests should have greater priority in influencing research commissioning;

- Future research commissions should build on existing evidence;

- Standards should be developed for the classification of research methods and reporting.

In a number of countries with highly regarded education systems, teachers are encouraged to be involved in research in a variety of forms. For example, according to Burn and Mutton (2014: 23): 'Finland can be seen as an entire integrated system in which teachers are regarded as researchers.' In Singapore there is 'a carefully planned and systematic attempt to create a culture of enquiry, critical reflection and deliberation within schools and classrooms in which teachers engagement with research (rather than active engagement in research) is deeply embedded' (Tatto, 2014: 18). Internationally the education system in both of these countries is seen as highly successful and governments across the world have been keen to copy aspects of good practice from Finland and Singapore. We do not have the evidence to support a correlation between research-active staff in schools and colleges and the relative success of their education system. However, it is significant to note that two of the most often cited, as effective, education systems in the world place a strong emphasis on the development of teachers and lecturers who have substantial research skills.

We would strongly advocate that all staff and students in schools and colleges have a role to play in developing 'evidence informed practice'. Encouraging teachers and lecturers to play a greater role in this process will increase the likelihood that changes to practice will be relevant to their classroom and properly embedded. Too often teachers and lecturers have complained about the latest fad or gimmick that is being imposed on them, often by central government. Evidence informed practice will give teachers and lecturers greater control over what happens in the classroom and enable them to test particular strategies. Greater engagement with and involvement in research will enable teachers and lecturers to take control of their own classroom practice and increase their direct influence on teaching and learning. Teachers and lecturers will therefore engage in research through making use of externally produced research evidence in their classroom or by carrying out their own inquiry in their own classrooms and in their own schools and colleges.

CASE EXAMPLE 6A

OUTSIDE HELP

Frances, headteacher of a large primary school which was part of an academy chain, had long been convinced of the benefits of getting her staff to engage with research findings, but, despite an open-minded staff, she had encountered significant resistance. The usual excuses were given by staff: lack of time, curriculum pressures, irrelevance, a perceived lack of expertise. The Academy chain developed a link with a local university to provide a bespoke MA programme for staff which had a particular focus on classroom-based research.

Frances saw her opportunity as she encouraged, especially through a time allocation, staff to join the programme. Quickly a research culture began to emerge which Frances supported by:

- Appointment of a research co-ordinator;
- Encouraging staff to feedback to others about relevant research;

- Devoting part of each staff meeting to the dissemination of research;
- Putting pressure on the Academy Chain to appoint a research director;
- Provision of a regular research bulletin;
- Instigating joint research-led sessions with other schools in the Academy chain to share good practice.

Francis was surprised at how quickly staff agreed to participate in a research-led approach. She said: 'It took the provision of time and some outside help, but staff quickly realised what was available would help the children they teach. I felt I was being left behind and staff were asking me what I'm doing. I've had to follow their lead and I'm now studying for an EdD investigating the development of a research led school!'

As we pointed out earlier in the chapter, one of the key issues surrounding educational research is that it is often perceived to be irrelevant to teachers and lecturers. By including teachers, lecturers and students into the group who are able to undertake inquiry we would argue that educational research will be perceived to be more relevant to the realities of the classroom. In the next section we will consider how we can develop models to facilitate effective classroom-based enquiry.

Models of good classroom practice

Throughout this book we have argued that professional learning and inquiry are positive factors that can contribute to improving outcomes for students. In practice, this will have to feed through into the classroom and the way in which teachers and lecturers work with their students. It is therefore essential that we identify a number of features that can contribute to the development of good classroom practice in professional learning and enquiry:

- *Training.* It is important that staff have the right mix of skills to be able to participate in inquiry. Many staff may have received little or no training in this area of activity and for others their skills may need refreshment and updating. Ensuring effective training at the outset will prevent many problems from occurring at a later date.

- *Time.* Teachers and lecturers complain that they have numerous demands placed on their time. Unless sufficient time is allocated to professional learning and inquiry, it will prove difficult to develop effective practice. A sufficient time allocation will have to be set aside.

- *Commitment.* There has to be clear commitment at various levels within the school or college. To give professional learning and inquiry sufficient value in the school or college, senior leaders have to endorse and support a structured programme. In addition there has to be equal commitment from all staff who fully recognize the potential benefits to classroom practice.

- *Leadership.* In addition to commitment from the school or college leadership, there have to be structures developed that identify who will take responsibility for professional learning and inquiry. This is necessary to develop and initiate projects, but also to ensure effective evaluation and reflection.

- *Support.* There have to be clear lines of communication and staff and students have to be clear about how they can access support for particular projects and who is responsible for providing support.

- *Status.* Professional learning and inquiry has to be given status within the school and not seen as a marginal activity. The support of senior leadership will be significant in ensuring this is given high status within the school or college.

- *Access.* Opportunities to undertake professional learning and inquiry have to be extended to all who interested in participating. This will include staff at all levels and students.

- *Resources.* The school or college will have to commit sufficient resources to enable a successful programme to develop.

- *Partnership.* Within the school or college there has to be a willingness to work in partnership. Partnerships can take a number of forms including internally with individuals and departments and externally with a range of outside organizations.

- *Safety.* All the participants in any professional learning or inquiry-based activity have to feel that they will not in any way be disadvantaged as a result of their participation.

- *Risk.* A culture that encourages risk-taking has to be fostered to enable experimentation to take place. The fear of failure has to be put to one side to develop a willingness to try new approaches.

- *Celebration.* Success should be recognized and celebrated through a series of activities supported by the school or college.

- *Review and evaluation.* Activities have to be subject to an effective and consistent review and evaluation procedure. This should be an open process and adopt agreed criteria. This process will enable decisions to be made about which projects are effective and where continuing support should be provided.

If sufficient thought and effort is not given to developing these features of good practice, there is a strong likelihood that initiatives to foster professional learning and an inquiry-based approach will fail. There will always be the lone member of staff who is able to influence professional practice and improve classroom learning. One teacher or lecturer can achieve a great deal but developing a culture of good classroom practice that permeates across the school or college will bring superior results. Having a coordinated approach will lead to greater opportunities and an increased likelihood of sustained improvements in teaching and learning.

Effective classroom inquiry

Having developed good classroom practice, what makes it effective? The ultimate test is what impact the inquiry has on classroom learning and student performance. There will be other outcomes that determine how effective the classroom practice has been. These include the impact on staff, replication and dissemination. However, there are a number of principles that underpin effective classroom inquiry and these include:

- Utilization of a range of different methods. It is important to recognize that inquiry can be used for a variety of purposes and should be designed to ensure them it is fit for purpose rather than following a particular approach. It is vital that those involved in the inquiry process should feel confident in using a range of enquiry methods.

- A contextualized approach that develops outcomes that are appropriate for the school or college should be implemented. The focus of the inquiry is likely to be a particular classroom or the wider school or college. Recognition of the contextual issues involved in a particular enquiry, and the development of methods that are consistent with the context will help to ensure successful outcomes.

- An evidence-based approach that leads to practical outcomes will encourage teachers and lecturers to participate in the process. Evidence should be clear and be presented in a manner that allows implementation in the classroom.

- Collaboration as a major feature of effective classroom inquiry. All participants should feel valued and involved in the process. It is important to ensure equal opportunities for participation between the various stakeholders: staff, students and researchers. They should also have appropriate involvement in dissemination and implementation strategies.

- Sufficient continuity of staffing to ensure that projects are properly completed, disseminated and evaluated. A high staff turnover will prevent the implementation of effective strategies to support improvements in teaching and learning.

- An emphasis on practice-based approaches to inquiry should be encouraged to ensure relevance. We will return to specific inquiry methods later in the chapter when we consider action research and practitioner research approaches in more detail.

- A focus on developing practical outcomes to the inquiry. The ultimate focus of any inquiry has to be to improve classroom learning and if teachers and lecturers are going to implement findings from a particular project they have to be convinced that they are practical and realistic.

- Develop accessible and clear materials based on the inquiry process. A variety of formats, including social media, can be used to ensure all participants have access to findings and materials developed from the enquiry.

Without proper support and commitment to these principles, it will be difficult to develop effective sustainable practice. This commitment and support has to come from all levels within the school or college. Co-ordination and leadership will be pivotal to ensuring that these principles are put into place and sustained. Individual staff have to recognize these principles and make them work in practice. In practice, a process of negotiation and consultation to ensure positive acceptance will need to be instigated by the school or college to ensure successful implementation.

Developing successful practice in an individual classroom is a worthwhile objective, but there are advantages to the development of models that can be more widely disseminated. The focus should not be solely on the individual classroom and there will need to be systems in place to ensure that a wider perspective is maintained.

Using research evidence in the classroom

There is a huge amount of research on education funded and carried out by a wide range of individuals and organizations. Ranging from international organizations to individual schools, from eminent professors to classroom teachers and lecturers, there is a constant output of research findings that take a variety of forms. For example, there are official reports, journal articles, books and websites all devoted to making educational research available to the academic community, parents, policymakers and the teaching profession. Yet how much of this output is actually read by teachers and lecturers and how much influence does it have on what actually happens in schools and colleges and the classroom?

Given the huge industry that is devoted to educational research, it would seem to be logical that schools and colleges make an effort to disseminate findings and provide opportunities for teachers and lecturers to access relevant materials in a systematic way. According to Sharples (2013) there is a need to develop a 'knowledge mobilization (KMb) ecosystem'. In this ecosystem research would become applicable and appropriate, through a process of negotiation and mitigation, for implementation by teachers and lecturers in the classroom (Nelson and O'Beirne, 2014). It is important to recognize that much of the research evidence that is produced is for a particular audience and may not be in an appropriate format for teachers and lecturers. There is a need to ensure that research evidence is fit for purpose to make it accessible to teachers and lecturers. It is unrealistic to expect teachers and lecturers to do this on their own and there is a need for the establishment of partnerships between the producers and the potential users of the research. It is interesting to reflect on how few universities have in place mechanisms to transfer their research into a medium that will be useful for practitioners.

Many teachers and lecturers have a commitment and belief in the benefits of using research evidence in the classroom. Much of what is produced is not immediately accessible to busy teachers and lecturers. There is a need to develop a mechanism that will adapt research evidence to make it more appropriate to the classroom. How many teachers and lecturers, for example, are aware of the major work into the way in which students learn that is being carried out as part of the emerging area of neuroscience? Schools and colleges have to adopt a number of strategies to facilitate improved use of existing research evidence in the classroom. These include the following:

- The development of partnerships with research-focused organizations to summarize and adapt research evidence. This is likely to be a university but could also include one of the many independent research organizations such as the National Foundation for Educational Research (NFER).

- Encouragement of partnerships with other schools and colleges to facilitate sharing of best practice.

- Provision of training to school or college staff to develop research skills, this may take the form of providing support for staff to undertake Higher Degrees. A number of Academy Chains and organizations such as Teach First and Teaching Leaders support teachers to obtain Masters level qualifications.

- The appointment of a member of staff to take the lead on research within the school or college. Many schools and colleges have appointed research officers who are given the responsibility of fostering increased use of research evidence in the classroom.

- Establishment of a mechanism within the school or college to filter and disseminate research evidence. A group of staff could take responsibility for this and make decisions about what is appropriate and develop protocols for the dissemination of research evidence.

- Disseminating research findings through a variety of methods. Examples include: provision of summary sheets, study groups, library materials, website, use of social media.

- Regular feedback from individuals and groups who have been making use of the research. This review process will enable decisions to be made about what is appropriate and what has actually had an impact in the classroom.

There is no hard and fast rule as to what will actually encourage and enable increased use of research evidence in the classroom. In practice it is likely to be a difficult process that requires long-term commitment from all those who are involved in the process. Inevitably there will be setbacks and obstacles in the way of progress. Levin et al. (2011) in a small-scale study in Canada has reported on the difficulties associated with trying to generate increased interest in and use of research in schools. In particular they comment on the how difficult it can be to change 'organizational behaviour'. However, they do acknowledge that there was much greater interest in the possibility of developing research and they identify the importance of key staff to act as a champion for research.

Where the interventions had the most impact, it was largely due to the presence of advocates and intermediaries or facilitators in the districts. In each of these cases a person or persons (usually one key person) led the way in supporting the intervention and in championing the increased use of research (Levin et al., 2011: 24).

The principles of action research

In the previous section we have considered the ways in which schools and colleges can make use of existing research to improve their own practice. In this section, we build on some of the issues raised in Chapters Two and Three to consider how teachers and lecturers can conduct their own inquiry projects into aspects of their own practice. This is becoming more significant in schools and colleges, as there is a growing acceptance that teachers and lecturers have key roles to play in bringing about improvements in student performance.

Significant numbers of teachers and lecturers are familiar with an action research approach. Many research methods programmes in education, including those in initial teacher education and post-graduate programmes, have a strong emphasis on action research and there has been a great deal published on this particular approach; see, for example: Altrichter et al. (2008); Koshy (2009); Townsend (2013). This approach has been gaining in popularity as schools and colleges take more responsibility for the development of their own inquiry programmes and encourage their teachers and lecturers to initiate inquiry projects. In practice, many teachers and lecturers feel more comfortable undertaking action research which they consider to be directly related to their own practice and can be seen to have an immediate impact on what is happening in their own classroom. The perceived relevance and relative speed of action research projects are attractive to teachers and lecturers.

According to Townsend (2010: 131) 'research concerned with practice needed to be based around actions'. Action research is associated with securing improvement in a school or college and especially at classroom level. It can be used in a number of different areas, for example:

- The development of alternative assessment and feedback techniques and systems;

- Developing alternative teaching approaches, including increased use of technology;

- Work structured around the development of learning skills and different types of learning;

- New approaches to classroom management and improved behaviour to facilitate learning;

- Improved administrative systems and protocols associated with issues such as attendance and punctuality; and

- Improved pastoral support and guidance systems.

The action research itself is usually structured around a series of cycles and this cyclical process should lead to improvements in the area of inquiry. A starting point for the person carrying out the inquiry is to undertake some reconnaissance into their chosen topic. As part of this process they would find out about the context and the focus of the research. This would enable identification of what needs to be changed and the development of a plan of action within an appropriate timeframe. An intervention in the classroom would take place and the actions would be put into practice. For example, this might involve using different teaching methods or making increased use of technology within the classroom. The impact of the intervention would be observed and then evaluated by the person carrying out the inquiry. If necessary, this process or cycle could be repeated with any changes in approach being reflected in the actions or intervention being undertaken. At the end of the process there would be a period of reflection and evaluation of any change or improvement that the actions had succeeded in bringing about. If the intervention results in improvement then the approach could be extended to other classes and tried by additional teachers. If there is no positive improvement the person leading the project might decide to try a different intervention.

It is worth noting that although the emphasis is on action, or doing something, the starting point of an action research project is to look at existing practice, reflect and then plan the action. Any action should only come after careful consideration of the existing situation and there should be an ongoing review of the activity. The temptation to rush into a particular action should be avoided and proper protocols should be established. The action or activity will be undertaken by practitioners and is part of a collaborative process involving teachers and lecturers as well as learners. Action research, therefore, directly impacts those who are involved in the process. Unlike other forms of research, that appear not to involve teachers and lecturers, action research is based on directly improving practice through controlled interventions and involving practitioners and learners in the process.

There are a number of issues surrounding the use of action research. In particular, given the particular context of action research, how relevant are the findings to another context? If the focus is on one particular classroom that is not an issue, but any attempt to broaden out the findings and apply them to another context might create some problems. There are also potential issues around impartiality and the ethics of 'trying things out' with particular groups. If the alternative is to do nothing and not address issues then, according to many teachers and lecturers, it is better to at least try something to change practice rather than accept the status quo. If proper procedures and systems relating to the development of effective practice have been put in place by schools and colleges there will be a clear mechanism to deal with some of these issues.

Although the emphasis is often placed on the individual classroom, in practice collaboration will be at the core of any action research approach. Action research can be an appropriate method to bring about significant improvements at classroom level and to ensure widespread staff involvement in the development of effective classroom inquiry. Teachers and lecturers should be encouraged to work together and more importantly to share details of their action research projects. Townsend (2010: 133) argues that 'action research is applied where people want to change something both as a result of and through their research'. There is little doubt that an action research approach will continue to play a major role in schools and colleges as teachers and lecturers take greater responsibility for improving their own practice and for wider institutional development.

Developing practitioner research

Despite the growth in popularity of action research in schools and colleges, as we have seen, it is not immune from criticism. Action research can be viewed as prescriptive and limited in scope with a particular process being clearly laid down that has to be followed. Clearly, in practice, there will be scope for adaptation and researchers will not always choose to follow the cyclical process we have described in the previous section. As a consequence we prefer the much broader term practitioner research which is not dependent on an intervention (Middlewood et al., 1999; Menter et al., 2010). We define practitioner research as 'all aspects of research related to your own practice in your own organisation' (Middlewood and Abbott, 2012: 88).

This approach offers greater opportunities to employ a variety of research approaches, but maintains the emphasis on improving effectiveness and practice in the classroom or more broadly in the school and college. Action research requires an intervention, this may be appropriate for practitioner research but conducting a data collection activity, for example, to develop evidence for the adoption of a particular strategy would be a legitimate form of practitioner research. Practitioner research does not require a direct intervention, but the findings from the inquiry may lead to changes in practice and hopefully improvements in performance. From a staff or student point of view practitioner research has a number of advantages:

- Any inquiry can be based on areas that require improvement in your classroom or more broadly in the school or college.

- The inquiry will be directly relevant to teachers and lecturers and potentially will lead to improved practice in the school, college or classroom.

- You will have a good insight into the particular area of inquiry because it is directly relevant to you.

- You will be aware of the background and the practicalities involved in undertaking the inquiry.

- You will be in a position to implement any findings relatively easily and quickly within your school or college.

There are a number of issues that teachers and lecturers have to consider if they adopt a practitioner research approach. There are the obvious ethical considerations which we considered in Chapter Four. Working in your own classroom or school and college requires you to maintain objectivity and to be aware of any potential conflicts of interest. Your inquiry might also generate data that is critical of your own practice or that of your organization. You have to be prepared for some unpleasant surprises and these may require careful and sensitive handling, especially when feedback is provided to other staff. Of particular concern might be issues that arise in relation to more senior staff. Again it is important that clear protocols are established and a sense of openness is encouraged by the school or college. In an ideal world, the area that you choose to investigate should be one that is of interest and relevant to you and your practice. However, there is a danger that your school or college might push you to conduct an inquiry that is important to the organization rather than to your own practice. Pragmatic considerations will have to be taken into account when undertaking practitioner research.

The major reason to undertake practitioner research is to bring about improvements in teaching and learning. Many teachers and lecturers would willingly accept an outcome that improved some aspect in their own classroom. However, practitioner research has the capacity to go beyond this rather narrow, but worthwhile, objective by developing models that can be more widely disseminated. According to Godfrey (2014: 16) there is a danger that a focus on this type of approach 'creates short-term fixes with little reach or impact'. In reality, many teachers and lecturers would opt for a short-term fix rather than settle for the status quo. However, the development of a model of good classroom practice should enable practitioner research to have a wider impact across the school or college and to bring about significant improvements in teaching and learning. Effective systems and protocols and careful identification of the issue to be investigated will enable practitioner research to go beyond the short-term fix.

CASE EXAMPLE 6B

GOING BEYOND SAFETY

Jane had recently been appointed as Head of Geography at an Academy School in the North West of England. She had been appointed with the brief to 'shake up the Geography department!'. The GCSE results were acceptable, but not outstanding unlike other curriculum areas, and there were only a few students going on to study the subject at Advanced level. She commented:

'I was aware there was a lot of traditional teaching and excessive use of the textbook by the established members of the department. I needed to do something to show alternative methods could work better so I decided to put to use my practitioner research skills I had developed on my recently completed MA course.'

Jane decided to use the classroom observation, of the teachers in her department, she had been asked to undertake to focus on teaching methods. This confirmed the impression of tired, dull but safe teaching. She also carried out a student survey to see what they disliked and liked about Geography and compared the findings from the other groups to those she taught. The results showed much higher levels of student satisfaction in Jane's groups compared to those of her colleagues. At the same time Jane undertook an analysis of student performance and her groups were outperforming those of her colleagues.

She shared her findings with the other members of the department and invited staff to observe her teaching in a more positive and interactive way. Jane also encouraged staff to communicate more through regular focused meetings and better sharing of resources.

The evidence supported what Jane was trying to do, but she was aware that it would take more to convince staff, who were interested but unsure about trying something new. She set up a student forum and asked them to undertake their own research to provide further evidence to staff. However she realized that staff also needed support and training to adopt new methods. Staff from the Geography department were encouraged to become part of a school-wide programme on teaching and development.

Regular monitoring with observation carried out by all members of staff has shown that teaching styles have been changed and student performance has improved. There has also been a slight increase in the numbers opting to study advanced-level Geography. As Jane commented, 'It hasn't been a total success but a small-scale project has impacted on teaching and learning. My staff are much more open to new ideas, without a focussed research project that would never have happened.' Jane has recently been appointed to a new post as leader of inquiry at her school with a specific responsibility to foster developments in teaching and learning.

Practitioner research has a broad context and can be adapted to the particular needs of a school or college or those of an individual member of staff. This is an obvious advantage and can play a significant part in encouraging staff to become involved in a wide range of research activities. Encouraging staff to adopt this approach in their classroom will provide opportunities to bring about significant change and improvement. There are obvious limitations, but used in conjunction with broader policies, to promote a research culture, practitioner research has the potential to enable staff to move from being on the receiving end of research to ownership and the producer of relevant evidence-based material. A comment by a further education lecturer we interviewed as part of our research for this book summarizes the positive benefits involvement in classroom-based research can bring:

> Doing a piece of research on the use of mobile technology has transformed my practice and given me a much better understanding of my students. What was especially good was being asked to present my work as part of a staff development day. It was never wracking, but my research manager helped me through. The presentation has been shared with our partner colleges and I've become a bit of a celebrity! I thought the principal didn't even know who I was, she does now!

Many teachers and lecturers are at the start of the journey to embrace a more research-focused approach to their work. In the next four chapters, we provide some examples where schools and colleges and their staff and students are well on their journey to create an organization that is based on professional learning and inquiry.

Summary of Chapter Six

This chapter has:

- stressed the role of professional development and inquiry in the development of effective classroom practice,

- put forward models of good practice of professional learning and inquiry that focus on the classroom,

- discussed the principles of effective classroom inquiry,

- described how to use research evidence in the classroom,

- outlined the principles of an action research approach in schools and colleges and

- described how practitioner research can be developed in the classroom.

PART TWO
Practice

CHAPTER SEVEN

The secondary school as research community

Richard Parker

Introduction

This chapter is an account of how one school set out to use practitioner research as a key driver to explore, evaluate and raise standards in teaching and learning throughout the organization.

The chapter:

- describes the context and overriding culture of the school,
- presents the rationale for introducing practitioner research,
- explores the principles and practicalities of using in-house research,
- outlines the nature and range of the research undertaken,
- considers its contribution to individual and organizational professional learning and CPD and
- assesses the impact on the teaching and learning.

The school's context and culture

As one of the very few remaining 14–19 community colleges in the United Kingdom, it was set up to provide educational opportunities for the whole community as well as operating as a multicultural comprehensive school for well over 2,000 students. The school is open from 7 a.m. until 10 p.m.

every week day and all weekends. It also runs five on-site businesses and offers educational provision for children as young as three months old (in its childcare centre) as well as adults well into their seventies and eighties.

Background

I was appointed principal in 2003 and came to the school already convinced by the power and influence of research on teaching and learning. In my previous headship, I had invited David Middlewood, then at the University of Leicester, to launch its very successful school-based Masters degree programme (which David had introduced and championed) into my then school, an eleven–eighteen mixed technology college in the East Midlands. The programme had been very well received and resulted in a significant number of staff achieving an MBA in educational leadership. I completed my Masters by the same route in 1997 and my subsequent experience as a research associate at The National College for School Leadership further convinced me that practitioner research could be a very powerful tool for improving and transforming schools.

Introducing practitioner research

Seeing people actively engaged in investigating, analysing and publishing their research findings on what makes for the best teaching and learning was powerful and persuasive. I knew then that in-house research could, if managed properly, be a highly effective agent for driving up standards and making all members of the organization much more reflective about their own practice and much less likely to become complacent! It did not, however (as I mention later in the chapter), make the contribution to the organization's day-to-day operations it could have done because, initially, we fell into the trap of not using the research findings to improve the school's overall quality of service.

The fact that the school had its own training centre and was already running university courses on-site for trainee teachers and teaching assistants made it ideally placed to promote the concept of the research-engaged school. The ethos was centred on three core principles:

- respect for all ('all different; all equal');

- rigorous student-centred aspirations and;

- a willingness to take risks if it looked like they would raise standards and expectations. One of the philosophies actively encouraged throughout the school was that it was better to fail magnificently than succeed cautiously!

This was vitally important because if practitioner research were to be introduced properly there would have to be a culture of mutual trust on the part of all those taking part. We were determined to open up research opportunities for all members of the college, which obviously meant that from the outset students, and support staff had to be involved as well. If there was any general sense of suspicion or indifference or, even worse, cynicism about what was being proposed there was no doubt in my mind that the initiative would fail.

The programme of in-house research was launched at the school in the summer of 2004 when students from schools in France, Sweden, India and Germany were invited to attend an international conference hosted by selected staff and students. During the conference, everyone involved had the opportunity to research a topic and report their findings in a number of seminars. The quality of debate was exceptionally high and the feedback strengthened our determination to place the concept of the research-engaged community at the heart of the college's learning culture.

The rationale for introducing practitioner research

For many years, academic research as such was not highly regarded by schools (Hargreaves, 1996). It was viewed as high powered, rarefied, inaccessible stuff that was light years away from the reality of life at the chalk face and hence largely irrelevant.

At a headteachers' conference in Cambridge in 1997, Hargreaves lamented the fact that academic research in education was costing the tax payer over sixty million pounds and the only people who were reading it were other academics. As a mechanism for improving standards in schools it was, he maintained, of no practical value or relevance whatsoever.

The same point was made in a research pamphlet produced by the National College for School Leadership (Sharp et al., 2006: 16): 'It is all too easy for research to become a private activity taken on by a few members of staff and of little interest to others.' Although classroom action research had been practised for some time (Elliott, 1984), this was essentially for individual teachers. School leaders needed to keep the focus on whole school engagement with research. This does not necessarily mean that all staff have to be actively involved, but it does mean raising awareness and making the research accessible to all.

I remember thinking at the time that the Masters degree courses I had introduced into my school three years earlier had provided the individuals concerned with excellent personal and professional development. However, listening to Hargreaves made me realize that all their research (and there was a great deal!) was lying on a shelf in the school library gathering dust.

It had, as Hargreaves had implied, made no impact on what we did at the school or how we were looking to raise standards. That was a salutary lesson for me, which profoundly influenced my decision to make sure that any research carried out would, if good enough, be made to work.

Launching the programme

These thoughts were uppermost in my mind when the leadership team made the decision to invest heavily in practitioner research across the school and, crucially, make it available to all staff and students who wanted to take on a research project. We really had to sell the concept hard and effectively. The central messages going out to staff from the leadership team were, therefore as follows:

1   We would remain wholly committed to the fact that in-house research can, if managed professionally and sympathetically, radically improve any and all areas of school life.

2   We believed that the inclusive culture at the school (a real strength) meant that any research would be viewed in the light of its quality and its findings and not by the age or the status of the person or group presenting it.

3   We were persuaded by the power, diversity and adaptability of rigorous research to analyse very broad or very specific areas of school life.

4   We were keen to ensure that any in-house research undertaken would be viewed as an opportunity to improve the quality of service offered at the school.

5   We were determined to ensure that the research was heard, acted upon and the recommendations, if sensible and worthwhile, implemented and subsequently reviewed.

6   We agreed that all the members of the leadership team at the outset signed up to carry out some in-depth pieces of research themselves.

In the three years after the scheme was launched, each one had carried out a piece of detailed research and four of them had completed Masters' degrees in educational leadership. Three gained distinctions! They also worked very hard encouraging other staff to consider taking first or second degrees and it was with some considerable pride that we managed by the end of the first year of the programme to have over 40 members of staff taking foundation, honours and higher degrees and sixty students enrolled on to the programme. Three years later, over twenty staff had graduated with Masters degrees and nearly fifty staff from our school, and from other schools in the county, had obtained foundation and honours degrees in teaching and learning.

The strength and impact of a development like this is hard to overemphasize. As Middlewood (2011: 16) points out, the research-based school is 'a recognition that improvement above all begins from within, not through the use of external consultants or experts but through the employees researching the organization's own way of operating'. The rationale for promoting practitioner research is also based on the reality that staff and students working in schools are intelligent, reflective professionals/aspiring professionals who are keen to discover for themselves what does and what does not work in the classroom.

The best practitioners will also want to find out how other schools and organizations have introduced high-quality practice in order to learn from their experiences and enrich their own as a consequence. Initially, such research – in the form of action research – tended to be confined to the classroom but as its popularity and relevance grew so it became a tool for analysing and improving practice in other areas of organizational practice and procedure. In this way, practitioner research became a mechanism for whole-school improvement.

The principles and practicalities of using in-house research

For the last forty years plus, schools have been bombarded by successive governments handing down diktats and policies from on high, that are presented as strategies to improve the quality of teaching and learning in our schools. Allowing senior leaders, staff and students to have the time, the support, the opportunity and the space to reflect on their own working practices will almost inevitably bear fruit. They can share their thoughts and ideas about the key objectives of their respective schools with their colleagues and line managers and explore initiatives that they believe will improve teaching and learning and raise overall standards. At one time, for example, we had a group of Year 10 special-needs students looking at the quality of school chairs and how they aided/impeded learning, another group of Year 12 students investigating the viability of introducing a house system into the college and two members of staff reviewing the college's data tracking procedures, with a view to refining and improving them.

Practitioner research: Key principles

It was clear to me that if we were going to introduce practitioner research effectively into the college, we would have to establish very early on certain key principles and then stick to them, namely:

- the opportunity to carry out a piece of research was open to all members of the college irrespective of age, educational qualifications and/or experience;

- the research would always have to be closely linked to the school's key aims and objectives, as set out in the college's corporate plan;

- any research carried out would need to be of a quality and rigour that demonstrated very clearly and persuasively that the outcomes reflected the evidence;

- all research would contain carefully thought through recommendations that would in turn be disseminated, analysed and, where appropriate, implemented;

- the recommendations implemented from a research project would be regularly and carefully evaluated and their impact on practice assessed.

Practitioner research – open to all

The title of this chapter has the word 'culture' in it – deliberately so. If the culture of the organization is exclusive, hierarchical and status-driven, in-house research will not work. Handscombe and McBeath (2003: 16) stress that a research-engaged school, if it is to be truly effective, must:

- have a research rich pedagogy

- have a research orientation

- promote research communities

- put research at the heart of school policy and practice.

For a school genuinely to become 'research engaged' it must therefore acknowledge that:

- everybody has the right to make suggestions as to how the place can improve

- everyone has the right to criticize constructively what they consider to be ineffective practice

- everyone needs to have the good manners and humility to listen to ideas that are put forward as ways in which to make things better.

The research-engaged school is no place for people who believe deep down that learning is best suited to a 'doctor/patient' approach to teaching where the teacher knows everything and the learner knows nothing.

Linking the research undertaken to the corporate plan

Making sure that all the research undertaken linked in to the corporate plan was a decision the leadership team took right from the beginning. As a result, all members of the organization were familiar with, and signed up to, the key aims and objectives of the corporate plan for that particular academic year. When a piece of research had been completed the person or group responsible would present their findings to the leadership team and any other members of staff who wanted to attend, and then outline their key recommendations.

The leadership team always followed up on their recommendations and let them know if and when they were being implemented. If the decision was that any particular recommendations were not deemed appropriate the reasons were always given. Every subject area had included in their annual development plan a column that identified which pieces of research had been carried out and what recommendations were being implemented as a result. At the end of each academic year those recommendations were evaluated in the light of their effectiveness/impact and then either removed (if those recommendations were time-bound or deemed to be unproductive) or carried over, realigned and/or updated as and when appropriate.

The research itself: Maintaining quality and rigour

It was clear from the outset that if the research being carried out was not of a high standard and failed to reflect the correct instruments and conventions of high-quality investigation, the findings would not be of any use. It was important that everyone understood what is meant by good research and that the senior leaders involved in the programme insisted on making sure that any research undertaken was relevant, worthwhile and valuable.

'Good research'

When Bauer and Brazer (2012: 4) state that 'school leaders must be both sophisticated critics of research to sort the good from the bad and, increasingly, producers of research knowledge to enhance their search for good solutions to the problems they face' they are of course making an important point. A clear definition of research (Johnson, 1994: 3) would maintain that it is 'a focused and systematic enquiry that goes beyond generally available knowledge to acquire specialized and detailed information, providing a basis for analysis and elucidatory comment on the topic of enquiry'.

Middlewood (2011: 19–20) suggests that all research should:

- be honest and use an ethical approach throughout

- have a clear purpose

- recognize its own limitations

- use the right instruments for the right purpose

- come to conclusions based on actual evidence

- make recommendations for action if possible, and

- enable the researcher to learn from experience and do even better next time!

Any organization contemplating becoming a research-engaged school needs to have these considerations at the centre of their thinking at all times. 'Rubbish in, rubbish out' is not just a warning for software programmers!

In-house research: Advantages and potential pitfalls

Giving people working in the organization the space and time to carry out pieces of research presents real opportunities and threats. People working in an organization will in all likelihood be very familiar with how things are and what they perceive to be the problems and even more significantly, the solutions. In-house researchers will therefore:

- find it more difficult to be as objective as an external person and instead lean more naturally towards subjective, anecdotal interpretations of facts;

- think that they already know how something could be improved;

- interpret people's response to questions/questionnaires in the light of what you consider to be true;

- avoid asking people to contribute to your research if they think they will disagree with your conclusions!

- alienate some staff who may already be very aware of how the researcher feels about a certain topic (particularly true where senior staff are concerned).

There are, of course, advantages as well. Knowing an organization will enable you to identify more easily and accurately what needs improving. Researchers will also know when and where to tread carefully and it is more likely that interviewees will be more forthcoming if they know and like the interviewer. Other major advantages include knowing who the 'movers and shakers' are, being familiar with how the organization operates on a day-to-day basis and, if you are a skilled negotiator, knowing that you should be able to persuade people more easily to complete questionnaires. It was imperative that everyone undertaking a piece of research received the right level and quality of training to ensure that the work they carried out was thorough and objective. Those staff involved in degree and post-degree work with our linked universities had more than enough expert guidance from their tutors to make sure that the research they undertook was of high quality. However, it was important that staff and students who were new to research had the appropriate levels of guidance and advice to help them carry out inquiries that would be valuable.

How to carry out research effectively

All students and staff who had little or no experience of carrying out a piece of research were given two full days' tutorial/workshop sessions at our partner universities – Leicester, Warwick and/or Nottingham where they learnt how to research a topic using established instruments and conventions. They were also taught how to avoid the most common pitfalls associated with superficial or ill-thought-through research projects. Areas covered included:

- how to construct effective and efficient questionnaires,
- how to decide which data to collect and how to collect that data efficiently,
- how to prepare for and manage interviews well and how to collate the data/information coming from them,
- how to avoid leading questions, double questions and over complicated ones,
- the use of research instruments such as observation, documentary analysis, shadowing, using diaries or logs,
- the use and impact of quantitative and qualitative research,
- how to arrive at the right question to ask when undertaking a piece of research and writing up the results/recommendations,
- how to write up and present research.

By insisting that all those considering carrying out some research had access to this training, many of the pitfalls associated with poor research were avoided. Unsurprisingly, the students who took part in the programme in particular, reacted very well to the university sessions and very rapidly became skilled research practitioners.

Researcher in residence

The other key decision taken by the leadership team was to commit some reasonably significant funding to the creation of a post that was deemed central to the operation of the research programme. We called the post 'Researcher in Residence' and allocated one full day a fortnight. Very occasionally, as the programme grew, we had to create more time to allow the tasks to be completed.

Key responsibilities of this new position included:

- chairing/presenting group sessions on practitioner enquiry,
- liaising with universities and co-presenting lectures on how to conduct research,
- one-to-one tutorials with staff and students (very important and very well received),
- targeted support for all those completing Masters' qualifications,
- leading the Leading Edge annual research conferences held at the school for all partner schools,
- marking assignments as and when required,
- liaising (as and when needed) with the leadership team.

This was a crucial appointment and getting the right person to do it would be a huge factor in deciding whether or not the initiative would be successful. We were very fortunate therefore, to secure the services of a very experienced university tutor who was also an acknowledged expert on practitioner enquiry, a highly regarded author of a large number of books on education and an experienced former headteacher who had enjoyed a long and successful career in schools before moving into higher education.

His contribution to the in-house research initiative was pivotal and the manner in which he carried out his duties central to the programme's success. All the feedback we received confirmed how important this role was, how much it fostered and maintained the right atmosphere for practitioner research to flourish.

Making the best use of the research

This chapter has stressed the need to make sure that any research carried out is of good quality and that every use is made of it. Therefore it was important that we kept a record of what research was being carried out and tracked its progress. With this in mind, we enlisted the support of one of the members of the Masters' cohort to take responsibility for coordinating the research (which included avoiding any unnecessary duplication) and tracking its contribution to the corporate plan. No one embarking on a piece of research could begin until this colleague gave him/her the green light.

All researchers were given considerable one-to-one support and guidance. We were also very clear that deadlines were expected to be adhered to. Any colleagues taking advantage of the Masters' degree qualification, which the college funded, only embarked on the course if there was a clear expectation that they were going to complete the course. Anyone leaving the course before completing the modules had to pay the incurred costs. By being fairly ruthless in this regard we created a culture of expectation that stressed that undertaking research represented a vitally important commitment to personal and organizational development and not to be taken lightly.

Presenting and disseminating the research

Every piece of completed staff/student research was presented to a panel that was made up of the leadership team, other invited senior staff/line managers and anyone else who wanted to listen to the findings. All recommendations were noted and put into an appropriate spreadsheet for further analysis. Whole-school research projects were considered by the leadership team and those recommendations that were going to be taken on board identified and disseminated. Every subject leader was expected to be present at any research work that affected his/her department. All departmental plans included a column that identified pieces of research that had been carried out and what recommendations had been implemented. These were discussed three times a year with the respective senior line manager.

The leadership team rightly judged that the more widespread and respected research became as an acknowledged and high-profile tool for school improvement, the higher its status would remain throughout the college. Having rigorous systems in place for coordinating, monitoring, reporting, disseminating and evaluating research was therefore of paramount importance. Each year the team responsible for managing the research programme across the college put in place evaluation procedures which assessed how effective the innovations arising out of the research had been and what modifications/amendments were needed. Some of the recommendations were time-bound and therefore, when the end date arrived, the innovations would either be shelved or adopted by the relevant staff/departments as agreed policy for the mid/long term.

The nature and range of the research undertaken

In the seven years from 2004 to 2011, in-house research became such an integral part of the college's operations and grew so quickly, that by the end of that period a vast amount of research had been carried out by teachers, students and support staff. A journal called *Professional Learning Matters* was collated and edited by two experienced researchers (neither of them, incidentally, qualified teachers!) and published three times a year. This journal highlighted much of the work that was being carried out and each year the Researcher in Residence hosted a research conference that provided a public platform for invited staff and students to present their research work and findings.

Practitioner research: The range and diversity

The real strength of any practitioner research programme is the flexibility and variety it allows for so many different people to become closely involved in whole school development. Research topics can be very wide-ranging and challenging, for example, 'investigating the benefits and disadvantages of moving to a vertical tutor model of student support' or they can be much more closely defined and much less complex, for example, 'investigating the popularity and nutritional value of college meals' or 'researching the benefits and drawbacks of whether to introduce a college radio'. In each case the conventions and the instruments need to be of the same quality and consistency as far as possible and if the recommendations are considered by the appropriate body to be worth adopting there should be an abiding commitment by the appropriate line managers to make sure that they are implemented.

A fairly short list of some of the research projects undertaken over those seven years illustrates the range and nature of the research carried out:

- Consider the impact of learning preferences in media and film;
- Do different chairs affect the levels of concentration in the classroom?

- To what extent are activities chosen for participation by Year 12 students influenced by those taken at key stage 4?
- An investigation into whether rewards given out by teachers have an effect on the attitude of GCSE students;
- To what extent can specific drama techniques used in Year 10 lessons enhance self-confidence?
- Managing change: A review of introduction of the college's extended day;
- Should the school have extended induction sessions for prospective external Year 12 students?
- How can the congestion in the corridors be improved?
- Promoting independent learning techniques in post-16 physics, using material differentiated by learning style;
- An investigation into whether visual displays in the corridors impact on students' experience of school;
- Does the seating arrangement in classrooms affect students' concentration?
- What impact have the changes in staffing in the premises department had on college practice?
- Identifying effective strategies to deal with challenging behaviour;
- Girls' preferred learning styles in English with specific reference to the novel 'Of Mice and Men';
- To what extent can the key concepts of the global dimension be integrated into the food technology curriculum?

When one notes the variety of areas covered in this list and then reflects on the fact that during the seven years the programme ran, well over three hundred pieces of research were completed, it is no surprise that practitioner research became such a powerful and well-regarded mechanism for improving standards throughout the organization.

Practitioner research: Its contribution to continuing professional development and learning

In-house research contributes to a school/college's professional development profile on three levels: the individual, the group and the whole organization.

At the individual level

The most obvious impact on the individual is the sense of achievement and self-worth that comes from completing successfully a demanding and complex research-based qualification. The looks on people's faces when they graduate eloquently reflect the time, energy and commitment that have gone into obtaining a degree while they are still in full/part-time employment.

Significantly, students are in my experience genuinely interested when they find out that one of their teachers is, like them, studying hard for a qualification and the fact that they emphasize to everyone in the organization that learning is lifelong and not confined to compulsory education. More experienced teachers have also admitted to me that when they submit a piece of work for marking, they are much more aware of how daunting it can be for students waiting for their work to be marked and returned!

There are other important gains:

- Developing the ability to analyse data, prepare good questionnaires, conduct interviews, write up the results and then argue the case for implementing the recommendations are all excellent skills for any teacher and/or student to have – and research provides all that and more.

- People who are taught how to research properly benefit greatly as a consequence: the conventions and instruments central to practitioner enquiry are extremely useful tools to apply to any situation which requires careful thought and analysis.

- Many students involved in the programme said that they became much better at finding good solutions to problems by utilizing the knowledge and skills they acquired carrying out their own research.

- Carrying out a piece of research builds confidence. Having the courage to identify an area of school life that could be improved, and then completing the research and presenting the findings provides excellent professional development.

- It really helps students! The parents of a Year 11 student whose research findings and recommendations had changed the way the school managed its transition procedures with feeder primary schools, said that their daughter had grown immeasurably in confidence and maturity as a result of completing and presenting her research.

- Anyone carrying a piece of research will almost inevitably meet with people from other departments, other areas of school life and establish contacts with a wide range of people that will help create and sustain a sense of collegiality throughout the organization.

At the group level

The most obvious impact is the fact that all those undertaking research will benefit and grow as a consequence from the peer support that almost always emerges within a group. During my first headship, there was a group of sixteen staff involved in the Masters' programme who had not attempted anything 'academic' for many years and who were frankly extremely apprehensive about taking on the challenges of studying for a higher degree. Seeing this group, seven of whom graduated at the same time, grow in confidence and develop a much clearer insight into the complexities of leading and managing a large organization was genuinely uplifting.

An additional benefit was the fact that many of the staff completing Masters degrees gained promotion to other schools or were appointed internally to more senior positions. Of course, all these staff had to meet other criteria to secure these promotions but there is no doubt in my mind that the knowledge and confidence they acquired from taking part in the research programme – and the dissertations in particular – made them much more marketable and likely to progress their careers as a result. Professional development that allows people to achieve promotion is good for the individual of course, but it also has a very positive impact on how people feel about a place that instinctively nurtures and supports ambition.

At an organizational level

A major gain for schools that embrace in-house research and have the confidence to make it widely available is that you open up exciting possibilities for the creation of new, dynamic partnerships. Being part of a group discussion between staff and student researchers who are exploring what makes for the best teaching and learning in an atmosphere of mutual trust and respect, has represented one of the real highlights of my time as a headteacher.

This sense of collegiality created by becoming a research-engaged school was well illustrated for me through an extended piece of research a group of students carried out on teaching and learning.

CASE EXAMPLE 7A

SHOWING THEIR TRUE COLOURS!

Six Year 11 students had for some time felt that the way the classrooms were set out, and the colour schemes on the walls (the traditional school colours of burnt yellow and burgundy) did not help the learning.

They also believed that the same colour scheme in the library and the way in which the books were displayed on the shelves deterred students from working there. The leadership team gave the group the time and some limited funding to carry out their research over the space of one term. The research centred on interviews with students, staff, caretakers and cleaners and the school business manager.

The premises manager was invited to work with the group and help them find out what colours and carpets were currently available to purchase from various suppliers. At the end of the term, the leadership team met with the students, the premises team and three of the cleaners to listen to the findings coming from the research and what the group's recommendations were. As a direct result of their research, the carpets were changed from burgundy to dark grey, the walls from burnt yellow to 'ice magic' (light grey!) and the layout of the library changed to one that all the students found much more friendly and welcoming.

The really uplifting aspect of this meeting was the fact that teachers, students and support staff all actively engaged in a discussion that was all about the quality of learning in the college and how it could be improved. It is difficult to envisage any other mechanism for raising standards being able to create such a dynamic mix of people and ideas. The students also had the real thrill of seeing the research they had undertaken making a direct impact on the teaching environment of the college and the premises knew that they were repainting the corridors and replacing the carpets for a reason!

Mention has been made in this chapter about the various ways in which becoming a research-engaged school can benefit all members of that organization. The following two case studies illustrate more specifically how practitioner research influenced the teaching and learning for the better.

CASE EXAMPLE 7B

GOING OUTSIDE THE BOOKS!

An English teacher in his second year of teaching carried out a piece of research to explore the extent to which conventional methods of communication encourage boys in key stage 4 to read for their own pleasure. Part of the research involved using Facebook with discussion forums and links to web pages on the set GCSE literature texts. Questionnaires were given out to find out how the introduction of reading logs, supervised quiet reading sessions, audio books and less well-known reading Internet sites had affected these boys' reading habits. The students who took part in the research were of different abilities and socioeconomic backgrounds.

The findings coming from the research suggested that non-conventional methods offer innovative ways of encouraging reading. The success of the audio books was very evident and the social networking sites that the students visited encouraged them to read more on their own. As a result of the research, the department decided to develop much more targeted technology to encourage reading and increase the use of audio books throughout the department. It was also agreed to introduce and promote the use of online blogs and discussion forums in the enrichment curriculum sessions.

The third case example concerns a group of Year 12 students who wanted to find out how effective the college's Virtual Learning Environment (VLE) was as a tool for promoting learning.

Case Example 7C

THE REALITY BEHIND VIRTUAL LEARNING!

The three Year 12 students used primary and secondary sources for their research. We sent out a large number of questionnaires to students in all year groups where they asked ten questions that were designed to assess how valuable these students found the VLE. They also interviewed those teachers who had had most direct impact on the VLE as it currently existed and a selected number of heads of faculties. The group also looked at a number of other schools' VLEs to find out how they were used and the extent to which they mirrored what was on offer at the school.

The results showed that some faculties used the VLE a great deal but a surprising number of staff hardly ever accessed it. The other worrying discovery was that although some students accessed the college's VLE to help their learning, rather too many used it as a diversion and an excuse to delay getting down to work. The recommendations put forward by the group were that the VLE should be used to support homework/revision/learning in a much more consistent, focused way than was currently the norm. All faculties were contacted and asked to make sure that the VLE was used as and when appropriate in their respective departments and the leadership team should as a matter of urgency introduce training opportunities for all staff in the most effective use of VLE.

The most valuable aspect of this particular piece of research was the realization that I and the other members of the leadership team had, prior to this group's findings and recommendations, thought that the school's VLE was a real strength of the teaching and learning provision and that it was being well and widely used. The students had of course picked up the fact that the people who told us that the VLE was providing such targeted and valuable learning support were the people who had developed it and were already willing converts. The research however had shown that many others at the chalk face were not. The recommendations were very quickly actioned and a whole school training day identified to address the major shortcomings the group had unearthed.

The enduring impact of practitioner research on teaching and learning

For too long, many schools have promoted an implicit culture that 'management knows best' and everyone else should accept they are in school to learn (i.e. conform). Others do not have a role to play in shaping policy, pedagogy or whole school practice. Built into this is a good deal of intellectual snobbery on the part of some school leaders who have on occasions been guilty of assuming that staff, and certainly students (!) are in no way equipped to comment on, nor be interested in, anything that evaluates the quality of service their respective schools are providing.

The situation is immeasurably better than it was, say, thirty years ago, doubtless helped by the growth of initiatives such as student voice and fast track qualifications for excellent teachers. However, as successive governments add pressure on schools to meet more and more ambitious targets or face the consequences, so school leaders may be less willing to allow staff and/or students the time and space to reflect on the quality of what is being done in their schools.

Becoming a research-engaged school challenges these fears and apprehensions head on. A major advantage of advocating and promoting practitioner enquiry is that by so doing, you encourage a collegiate sense of responsibility for what goes on in the classroom and elsewhere in the school. If you ask children from foundation stage upwards to comment on what they like or do not like about their school, they will always provide you with some useful insights that will help improve things.

If you ask sixth formers to help you evaluate the quality of learning in the classroom, they will relish being asked to take part and more readily appreciate the professionalism and commitment of their teachers and as a consequence, be much more appreciative of what they do. When teachers and support staff become involved in practitioner research, they will invariably identify much more directly with the school's core aims and objectives.

In-house research, if it is be of any lasting value, will have to impact directly on the quality of teaching and learning in a school. If it does not, then it becomes little more than an expensive intellectual exercise which may well be of some interest to the individual engaged in it, but of little real value otherwise. Middlewood (1999: 135) quotes a programme manager in a secondary school saying, 'In the end, everything comes back to teaching and learning. That's what the school is ultimately judged by, that's what makes the daily job fulfilling or not for staff. Every outcome from research here eventually will have some implication for how we teach and learn here, and the better we do both, the better we'll get.'

Aspinwall and Pedlar (1997: 230) suggest four different types of learning in an organization:

- learning about things

- learning to do things

- learning to become ourselves, to achieve full potential

- learning to achieve things together.

Schools have traditionally been engaged very clearly in the first two types of learning and far less on the third and fourth. Even now, the focus is far too much on the acquisition of facts at the expense of real learning!

Introducing practitioner research into a school so that it becomes truly 'research engaged' will, I am convinced, enable schools to find more time and space to recognize and develop Aspinwall and Pedlar's third and fourth types of learning. If you ask a member of staff or a student to carry out a piece of research for you and report back the findings with a view to using those findings to improve practice, you are, in effect, paying them a real compliment. Put simply, you are showing that you rate their intellect, you trust their professionalism and you value their opinions.

Conclusion

This chapter has stressed how research, if managed properly, can benefit the individual and the organization in equal measure. Those people carrying out pieces of research into how a school operates and how it could improve its practice will always learn something about their own approach and philosophy to teaching and learning while at the same time making a valid contribution to whole school improvement.

In this way, everyone in the organization will develop a clearer understanding of how and why things are as they are and where their own particular contribution and expertise fits in. One Year 13 student commented on how completing a piece of research into how to make the

Year 12 biology modules more accessible and user-friendly changed his opinion of the learning culture at the college. 'I now realize,' he said, 'that in our school it is not a case of the teacher teaching and the learner learning. We are all learning.'

There is no doubt that establishing a culture of practitioner research will present schools with real challenges. There will be some staff inevitably who will resist the chance of somebody looking closely and systematically at the work they do in the classroom. Some will still believe that students are there to listen and not question the validity of what is done. However, the benefits far outweigh the negatives. Practitioner research is not hierarchical; it is not unfairly selective and does not require a hatful of academic qualifications for it to be carried out well. By establishing a culture of practitioner enquiry I have no doubt that everyone benefited significantly as a result and the impact and influence on the teaching and learning made the place a much more rewarding and dynamic environment in which to work.

Summary of Chapter Seven

This chapter has:

- described the reasons that committed the school to in-house inquiry,
- identified the features of the school's development,
- explained the factors in the school's success in this field,
- given examples of the various in-house inquiries and
- commented on the impact on the school's culture and overall development.

CHAPTER EIGHT

The primary school with CPD at its heart

Sue Robinson

Introduction

This chapter is an account and discussion of how an integrated approach and commitment to professional learning or continuous professional development (CPD) at Forest Primary School led to whole school improvement in standards, high retention levels of staff and an outstanding judgement from Her Majesty's Inspector (HMI) in 2009 for leadership and professional development.

The chapter:

- describes the context of the school,
- identifies issues which needed to be addressed,
- outlines ways in which professional development needs were identified, structured, monitored and evaluated for impact and
- draws out the underlying principles involved the vision and strategy for developing professional learning.

The context of Forest School

Forest School is a large two-form entry over-subscribed primary, with a Nursery and a Children's Centre attached. It is situated in an area of high deprivation in the English Midlands. There is a wide diversity of intake with children drawn from different minority ethnic backgrounds. In 2011–12 percentages equated to approximately 35 per cent Indian, 25 per cent Pakistani, 20 per cent African-Caribbean and 20 per cent other, mainly dual heritage, backgrounds.

Children identified with special needs requiring either a statement or school action and school action plus averaged around 15 per cent and between 18 and 20 per cent were in receipt of free school meals (FSM). This is not to be confused with those entitled to FSM but chose not to register as they chose not to access them, many of whom went home at lunchtime.

Attainment on entry, baselined at Nursery was below national averages and there were high levels of English as an additional language. Achievement and attainment were both high and considerably above national averages with statistics illustrating improvement in five-year trends in attainment and progress. From a baseline of below average compared with national age-related bands, standards by the end of Year 6, and value-added trends with 100.0 as average, showed an increase: 2008 – 100.6; 2009 – 101.0; 2010 – 102.0; 2011 – 102.0. By 2011 the school was in the top 4 per cent nationally for progress in English and Mathematics. Key Stage 2 results for L4+ in English and Mathematics were consistently between 92 and 97 per cent. The actual results at end of KS 2 with Level 4 for being an average for age 11 in 2011 were English L4+ 95 per cent and L5 42 per cent and Mathematics 92 per cent L4+ and L5 43.5 per cent.

The staffing structure reflected the years spent supporting other schools and the need to have capacity to ensure leadership in the absence of staff while they were supporting other more vulnerable schools. The school employed a deputy at 0.6 as a support school deputy. Staffing included:

Teachers (19):

Headteacher,

Deputy Head and curriculum leader,

Support School Deputy Head (0.6) from 2009,

3 Assistant Headteachers (Phase leaders, EYFS, KS1 and KS2, with additional responsibilities for Assessment, English, Mathematics and Citizenship),

Senior Teacher for Inclusion.

5 Middle Leaders for each curriculum group across the school:

Creative Arts,

Humanities and Science,

RE and personal and social education and

PE and Health Education.

Special Needs Coordinator (SENCO),

7 class-based teachers with no additional responsibility but who were members of the Creative Arts, Humanities and Science, RE and personal and social education and

PE and Health Education faculties.

Teaching support staff (14):

1 teaching assistant in each class from Nursery until Year 3 and then 1 teaching assistant per year group, plus a teaching and learning mentor who supported children with emotional or behavioural needs;

2 nonclassed-based teaching assistants.

Nonteaching support staff:

3 admin staff at various levels;

1 School Business Manager who also worked across the Children's Centre;

1 School Premises officer.

The Children's Centre was led by a manager who also had qualified teacher status, with support from 2 admin assistants and 4 development workers.

A key feature of Forest School, for which it received wide acclaim, was the emphasis it placed on citizenship and a personalized curriculum and individual pathways of learning. Children devised their own published 'Children's Charter' for the school. They were given many opportunities to represent the school such as: Young People's Parliament; Young Leaders projects; Music projects, representation at workshops for the SSAT (Specialist Schools and Academies Trust) and BECTA (British Educational Communications and Technology Agency). The school was proud of its wide-ranging activities and awards of which examples included: Investors in People, Active Mark Silver Eco Award, Basic Skills Quality Mark, Healthy Schools Standard, Leading Aspects for Citizenship and Assessment, School Achievement Awards, 'School for young citizens', BECTA and also that it became a National Support School in 2007.

The historical context

In 1996 OFSTED (Office for Standards in Education) identified Forest School as having not only strengths but also some significant weaknesses. It was shortly afterwards that the writer was appointed as headteacher. One of the saddest days of her life was the first staff meeting when she asked everyone to be honest about how they felt and how collectively they could address any issues from the inspection. There were many people upset at that meeting and the writer left with an overwhelming feeling that not only did the school need to improve education for the children but also the morale and self-esteem of the staff. Only then could they build the skill level and capacity of the staff, that is, their professional learning, and thereby begin to improve the standards of the children's work and their well-being.

From that day the head set about developing a climate of trust where all would be heard and all ideas welcomed and considered. Forest would become outstanding, not because it complied with an artificially created inspectors' tick list but because the people who worked there and sent their children there, believed it to be.

The next section of this chapter illustrates how, with the support of the staff and community at Forest, it was judged to have made excellent progress by 1999 and highlighted as such by OFSTED in its report of that year and again in 2004. Subsequent OFSTED inspections made similar judgements and the role of CPD was identified as being integral to the judgement of outstanding for leadership in 2009.

The system for staff's continuous professional development is of high quality. There are clear pathways and regular opportunities for all staff to develop their leadership skills with external providers and the school's own programme for staff development.

Developing professionally

Professional development as it existed at Forest in the late 1990s tended to be functional. It was useful in that it offered training in how to manage the standardized tests or health and safety but it did not consider how to provide for members of staff who were reflective and had a deep understanding of pedagogy. There was no opportunity at that stage for peer-to-peer support, or post-graduate learning supported by the school.

Staff development in pedagogy and the curriculum tended to be in small, unconnected and poorly disseminated day courses for those who were responsible for an area or who had the loudest voice when asking. There was no coordinated or budget-based approach to identifying need through a skills audit and a self-review.

Starting almost from scratch as it seemed then, a way had to be found to motivate staff and to listen to them. One of the first opportunities offered was to 'Invest in People'. This was the first time the school had systematically sought the views of the staff on its effectiveness and asked them what they believed were their professional development needs. It was aligned then to a skills audit and the first embryonic attempt to produce a skills directory for the school which was then matched to professional development opportunities. Forest continued with the Investors in People initiative for some years and became benchmarked at the highest level.

Parallel to this was the early appraisal system which was the forerunner to performance management. While it was statutory, many schools were largely ignoring it. At Forest, the leadership used appraisal as a mechanism to identify staff development needs. However, while following a formal appraisal system for performance management, the school also retained the personal development, individual conversation the head had with each member of staff. While time-consuming, it was considered to be particularly beneficial for building trust and relationships. Training and development was a twin track of self-review by the staff, together with training identified through audit and the monitoring and evaluation systems of the school.

Allied to the issue of some poor-quality teaching was some poor-quality learning. It was argued at the time that much of the latter was due to a curriculum which was taught in discrete subject areas and according to a syllabus which it was felt did not cater enough for the needs and interests of the children or show sufficient linkage between skills and application.

As staff became more skilled, the school also developed the curriculum. It was based on an individualized approach tailored to the interests and needs of the children in the belief that a curriculum which concentrated particularly on teaching to the tests at end of Key Stage was counter-productive. It was boring and demotivated the children, as well as the staff who were teaching it. This approach having been adopted, a successful inspection in 1999 gave staff the confidence to change radically. The curriculum was redesigned primarily to ensure creativity and engagement, with a balance between knowledge- and skills-based teaching and learning and when inspected in 2004 and again in 2007 was judged to be 'excellent' by OFSTED.

A personalized curriculum required a high level of skill from the teaching and teaching support staff as a lot of the planning and assessment was in the hands of the teachers. A framework for the curriculum was devised but planning and lesson content was left to teachers with guidance from middle leaders but not heavily prescribed in detail by the senior leadership team.

A system relying on the skill level of class teachers and middle leaders needed to be accompanied by a level of trust. If staff were to be given a high degree of autonomy through distributed leadership it was also essential for them to have high levels of understanding and skill in what constituted high-quality teaching. If staff are to be held rigorously to account through performance management and standards then it is fair for them to expect a high level of professional development to improve their professional learning.

One measurement of the success of this strategy is that the school was judged outstanding for professional development and distributed leadership and high levels of trust by HMI in 2009.

The school's work to develop the skills and effectiveness of leaders is outstanding. You have successfully created a common vision based upon a belief that the key to school improvement is the effective distribution of leadership and the development of leaders at all levels.

To complement these judgements, the school also received consistently outstanding judgements from the Local Authority's external evaluation through the use of the School Improvement Partner audits as the following show:

> All contributing individuals [Forest] are valued' . . . Regular and focussed CPD opportunities for a complete range of staff and stakeholders . . . Systems are rooted in evidence and promote professional development . . . Evidenced by the number of very effective senior and middle managers who are home grown . . . [Head] also empowers others through meaningful delegation and allows them to take the credit for successes.
>
> School Improvement Partner (2011)

This chapter now moves to a more detailed description of the system of audit and evaluation which underpinned the school's vision for professional development of staff and its overall effectiveness.

Steps to planning, implementing and evaluating a strategy for successful professional learning

To address the issues outlined earlier the school set about creating a 'learning organization' which aligned with the following definition:

> While traditional organisations require management systems that control people's behaviour, learning organisations invest in improving the quality of thinking, the capacity for reflection and team learning, and the ability to develop shared visions and shared understandings of complex issues.
>
> (Senge, 1990: 287)

The school devised a learning (CPD) team, the role of which was to ensure that the aim of balancing the individual requirements and requests of each member of staff with those of the school was a fair and equitable process and met the needs of both as far as possible.

The team consisted of a representative from the different categories of staff including the school business manager, and led by an assistant headteacher. It was important to have a team which reflected the different aspects of the school team because between them they would be able to represent the vision of the organization, the values which underpinned the overall vision and provide the strategy to translate it into action utilizing appropriate resources led by the business manager. How this purpose was translated into action is described in the rest of this section.

Identifying need

Auditing strengths and weakness in the provision of education and the requirements for future provision was a key feature of the school. It was important not only to identify practice but also to have the mechanism to address issues as they arose and not just at the end of a cycle.

Various audits were used which included whole school reviews, review of individuals and external review.

Whole school audit included:

- The needs of the school identified through the School Improvement Plan (SIP), regularly reviewed,
- Quality of teaching reviews related to children's progress,
- Books scrutiny,
- Formative assessments of children's achievement and attainment and related pupil progress meetings,
- Evaluations by pupils.

Review of individuals:

- Targets identified through individual members of staff's self-evaluation,
- Performance management to identify need and structure support,
- Classroom observations by senior staff,
- Peer observation.

External and stakeholder reviews:

- OFSTED and other external reviews such as the School Improvement Partner,
- Summative assessments of children's achievement and attainment at end of Key Stage,
- National and local priorities – for example, Primary Strategy,
- Feedback from stakeholders, parents, pupils and governors.

In-house identification of professional learning needs

It can be seen that the above included both internal and external processes, both more formal through generally used management processes, and more personalized, targeted ones. Since the internal and more personalized ones are most relevant to the overall theme of the book, more details are now given of these.

Pupil involvement

Forest's mantra, identified in its mission statement and the introduction on the website, was that 'Children are the heart of everything we do'. Therefore their opinions in various forms were sought and used to feedback to staff, parents and governors. Curriculum topic areas were always started with an exercise geared to determine what children knew about a particular area and what they wanted to find out. This was captured simply on 'post- its' and left on the appropriate wall area in the classroom. At the end of the modules of work children were asked a similar question about what they felt they had learned and what had helped them to learn. This became part of the school's curriculum monitoring by middle leaders.

Pupil voice was an integral part of the school's structure. Children contributed to a range of aspects of school life, for example, house captains, play buddies, ICT (Information Communications Technology) buddies, the school newspaper, helping to design the website and many other roles of responsibility. A 'house system' with representatives from each year group and school council ensured a feedback process to the senior leadership team. This was managed by an assistant headteacher whose role was pastoral and personal, health and social education (PHSE) and citizenship. It was on one of these occasions that changes to the school's website was debated as described in the following case example.

CASE EXAMPLE 8A

NOT TOO YOUNG TO KNOW!

The Senior Leadership Team (SLT) met with the School Council on a regular basis usually once per half term. It was from one of these conversations that we agreed with the School Council that the website was 'tired' and in need of review. The website was viewed as the way the school could communicate to those outside who may be interested in the work and life of our school. We were proud of it and updated it regularly. However staff also agreed that the format needed updating.

The School Council was charged with the task of coming up with amendments agreed by the children. They collated the views of children in each year group about what they liked and wanted to see and what they thought could be changed. Council members were surprising in that an interesting aspect for them was the publication of tests' results, perhaps because the standards were high and they were proud to advertise the fact. Apart from statutory requirements they were quite happy for all data to be published. There followed from this an interesting discussion about confidentiality and data protection.

Following the gathering of data, the School Council devised changes to the site. These changes were shared in the SLT meeting. Some time was spent looking at what the site would look like with different formats. Changes included the organization of the site to include more photographs and links to the classes, which were then to be responsible for the content and update of their section of the site. In addition, the whole feel and atmosphere changed through the use of a different font and colour scheme.

What struck the staff particularly, was that while they felt the children might prefer to see bright primary colours and a rainbow they discarded this notion as unsophisticated. Their preference was to use black, red and grey as the main colours due to their views that this would be more 'business like'. What was impressive was the careful consideration given to the task and often sophisticated ideas and technological knowledge of the children.

Pupil questionnaire responses showed that children showed great enjoyment of learning. One comment 'we have more opportunities to learn outside the classroom and can write from "real life" experiences' demonstrated a recognition of the change in focus in moving to a more integrated and experiential form of learning.

Children commented that they enjoyed their parents working and learning alongside them in school, for example in INSPIRE workshops, assemblies, trip feedback, parents who support reading. Extra-curricular clubs were oversubscribed and many of these ideas for school improvement came from meetings with the pupils held by the assistant headteacher and, where possible, the headteacher.

Classroom observations

Observations took place in a variety of ways and degrees of formality. Perhaps the most effective from the point of view of the writer is the informal, incidental monitoring gained through walking the site, visiting lessons, discussions with individuals. In addition were the formal observations to inform performance management and those where middle leaders monitoring their areas would join lessons and discuss the completed work. This would inform their reports but was not a part of formal lesson observations. In addition, staff offered demonstration lessons which were observed by those who took advantage of the offers in the menu of opportunities already described for those who sought advice from other staff about a particular aspect of their work.

Feedback from others

Other feedback came in the form of external feedback and review. In addition to the school improvement partner or other external reviews, governors were all involved. They were members of one or more committees such as curriculum or pastoral and each would be linked to a subject area. They would meet once per term with the leader of a designated area in school and would look at work (anonymized) and speak to the children. They were encouraged to write their findings for governor's reports but their feedback was mainly verbal.

Parents too indicated their satisfaction with the school's approach as demonstrated by these examples from parent questionnaires:

- 96 per cent of parents felt that their child finds the work stimulating and challenging (2010);

- 100 per cent of parents are satisfied that their child enjoys being at school (2011).

Professional development plans

Stakeholder voice was used as part of the audit process for the SIP. This included using what had been learned to review how the school plan should be amended in a year, and for targets and development for the next year. In addition, a training plan was prepared including costs, based on requests for professional development and as a result of data derived from the audits outlined above. The training plan became an annexe to the SIP which was distributed to all stakeholders and discussed at staff and governors meetings.

Professional development opportunities would include opportunities for individual staff and whole school development needs. Professional development needs would form part of the SIP but were reviewed during the year. In this way the school could remain flexible and address need as it arose.

Some professional development was whole school and was identified because of a change in government policy such as that which formed the literacy and numeracy strategies or changes to the National Curriculum. Other needs were individual. These could be because of a gap in subject knowledge identified as an individual need or a wish to develop as a leader of a subject or part of an induction process for new teachers.

CASE EXAMPLE 8B

PROFESSIONAL LEARNING FOR STAFF RETENTION

Karina was an assistant headteacher at Forest and an example of the active process undertaken for retention of high-quality staff.

She joined Forest School as an NQT. As part of her induction process and sessions with her NQT mentor, Karina was quickly identified as someone with potential for leadership.

Karina was very modest in her recognition of her achievements at first and was almost disbelieving at the feedback she got from observations of her teaching and the evaluations of her NQT targets. Encouragement was needed through pastoral interviews with the headteacher for Karina to see herself as a future leader.

It was the policy of the school to 'grow our own'. The reasoning was that it was a way of retaining and developing talent. As part of this process Karina's first promotion came as the school began to form a 'faculty' approach to the curriculum and to group subjects and teams to lead and manage them. Karina became a middle leader for PHSE and Citizenship and was responsible for developing pupil voice in the school. It was decided to develop these areas further and to become more outward-facing as a school becoming involved, for example, in Young People's Parliament activities, interschool debates and producing a Children's Charter designed by the pupils and coordinated by Karina.

The school governors agreed to fund post-graduate study as a form of retention for staff who requested it and who had a positive performance management review. From the beginning it was clear that Karina would be interested in this and to develop her pedagogy in terms of the pastoral side of education and the role of pupils in the wider effectiveness of the school. She was funded to undertake an MA and encouraged to continue when her personal circumstances meant she had to defer.

When Forest became a National Support School and the senior leadership was involved more often working in other schools, Karina applied for and was appointed to the role of assistant headteacher. Her areas were the same as those she had undertaken as a middle leader but in addition included community cohesion and behaviour. The school not only wanted to retain her but also to accommodate her desire to stay in the school and lead within it rather than as part of the support school team. In this way the school acknowledged the different talents of its staff and accommodated them as a means of retention.

Whole school development once identified and incorporated into the SIP was mainly delivered in-house or by trusted external providers and presented in staff meetings/whole staff training days and, less likely, on individual courses.

Individual development needs could be addressed by:

- Menu of internal professional learning opportunities;

- Working to support in other schools as part of building capacity in base school;

- Post-qualification study to include teachers, teaching and non-teaching support staff. Examples being Certificate and Diploma of School Business Management (C/DSBM) MA and EdD or PhD, National Vocational Qualification (NVQ) levels for teaching assistants and various levels for children's centre staff including National Professional Qualification for Children's Centre Leadership (NPQICL) and middle and senior leadership accreditation to include the National Professional Qualification for Headship (NPQH).

Some of the popular and effective areas for development are described in more detail.

Staff attending courses and conferences run by outside agencies

Staff could request professional development through their performance management targets. They could also be provided with training through identified professional needs and from areas identified in the current school improvement priorities. Details of all courses that were available, and those courses attended were kept by the CPD leader. The school expected the dissemination of good and successful CPD practice but that could be supported by audits of practice and it was not expected that there would be feedback from every course undertaken by an individual. A budget was allocated for course costs.

Development offered outside the school day but within school

In-school development was organized on a termly basis. There were regular requirements that appeared annually, such as book sampling, parent's evening workshops, target-setting booklets, INSPIRE parental workshops preparation time, focus week planning. Other sessions were chosen according to the immediate needs of the school as identified by audit.

Providing development and consultancy for other schools

The staff at Forest School had been involved in training colleagues from other schools since 2002. This initially started through several staff being chosen as 'Leading Teachers' in Mathematics and English and involved staff going out of schools and leading meetings or team teaching or colleagues coming to Forest School for shadowing teachers, meeting and so on. From 2002, the head teacher's involvement in working in other schools began with an invitation to support a head teacher new in post and experiencing difficulty in another school.

Post initial qualification study

Many staff chose to study in their own time to gain further qualifications which had been identified as those the school wished to support professionally and financially. These were diverse and included: netball coach certificates, Masters Degrees, NPQH/NPQICL and NVQs.

One of the key features of some of these programmes, especially the Masters, is to enable participants to undertake in-house research. Two such examples are:

1 Mary carried out an investigation into the effective leadership of team meetings. Using observation (with agreement) and semi-structured interviews with a sample of team leaders, she found a set of criteria that became the norm. Although these criteria were not in any way revolutionary, the important factor was they were agreed through the research. This meant that consistency became the key factor in the way meetings were led, so that whichever meetings someone attended, they could be confident of the same effectiveness and thus there was less time-wasting and frustration, and more agreed outcomes. As noted, even though the criteria could almost have been listed in advance (everyone having a say, good timekeeping, etc.), the value lay in the fact that people's views had been professionally and academically sought, thus gaining consensus.

2 Jean investigated the collaborative relationship in class between teacher and teaching assistant. Using interviews with a sample of both teachers and assistants, some inconsistencies were revealed. There were even situations where teacher and assistant gave quite contrasting accounts of operations which both were involved in. This led, fortunately, to a good deal of laughter rather than tantrums! This perhaps says something about the climate of trust that had developed to enable such research to take place. Certainly, in the early days described above, such goodwill would not have been possible. The outcomes of this investigation led to greater openness in those relationships as well as specific actions such as agreed brief feedback chats between teachers and assistants at regular set times.

Each of these examples, plus others, directly led to professional learning within the school where a need had been identified. The former led to an in-house presentation to team leaders and all team members, while the second resulted simply in teachers and assistants, chatting and 'passing the word around', so that practice gradually became affected as others found it useful.

Deputizing/distributed leadership

Many leaders gained the opportunity to develop professionally through deputizing for colleagues in planned or unplanned absences. Planned absences included staff working in other schools as part of the National Support School role. Their role in the base school needed to be covered often with a team approach to ensure that capacity was built and standards maintained and improved in their absence. Many more inexperienced staff gained a valuable insight into leadership from this supported approach to stepping up to a leadership role.

Peer supervision/mentoring

Staff provided support and guidance to new staff or staff that had changed year groups or role responsibilities. It was expected that the more experienced teacher would guide and support their colleagues in the routines and expectations of the school and a specific year group. This was often valuable early experience of leadership.

Training/coaching/development given by colleagues within school or from other schools

One of the most successful initiatives was the introduction of a variety of internal professional learning opportunities that was made available to staff. This was developed as part of a response to audited need from the monitoring and evaluation of teaching and learning and performance management. The leadership at Forest School also became aware that as they were used extensively outside their own school, staff were gaining particularly useful skills and knowledge and it would be useful to share that internally.

Together with skills gained externally the leadership wanted to share those areas of expertise that existed in school about which they were less aware. An example of that was the dramatic expertise of one member of staff and musical abilities of another. A list was compiled by asking staff both what they would like support to improve and what they felt they could offer in support to other members of staff. One key to the success of this strategy was that it worked to support across teaching and non-teaching staff. Requests could include coaching, demonstration lessons, language support, inclusion strategies, data handling and behaviour management as examples. The list was compiled and monitored by the CPD leader and evaluated in terms of its access and the effectiveness of the ways in which concerns and requests were addressed by the CPD team reporting to the head teacher and governing body.

In addition, staff had the opportunity to work closely with two local specialist secondary schools. They funded teachers work with Forest staff both in class and specifically with training how Forest's staff taught specific areas of the curriculum to reach high levels of attainment in Maths, French, Science, Gymnastics and Athletics.

Succession planning career planning

Through performance management, overall strategic planning, and the ethos of the school, individuals' career development was identified, supported and developed. Strategic staffing changes in year groups and curriculum areas were planned strategically and leadership courses identified and budgeted. These opportunities took the form of an identified programme such as Tomorrow's Leaders Today (National College) for those in the early stages of leadership development or leading from the Middle and Leadership Pathways for those in middle leadership and senior leadership positions. In addition, Forest offered coaching for leadership.

Evaluating impact

The impact of any professional learning was assessed as appropriate. Individual assessments and evaluations of particular opportunities were fed back to the professional development leader shared with the team and the overall quality of professional learning was discussed as part of the senior leadership meetings. Usually this meant a quick resume of activity or a report of anything which needed action to praise or improve. In addition the professional development leader reported termly to the governing body. The report commented on:

- Pupil attainment
- Improved teaching and learning
- Increased pupil understanding and confidence
- Increased evidence of reflective practice
- Recruitment, retention and career progression

Newly qualified teachers

In addition to the above newly qualified teachers (NQTs) had a structured programme closely linked to their professional learning needs. It included an entitlement to a professional induction period, and development based on:

- An assurance that NQT mentors would receive up to date training and had clear roles and responsibilities and these would be reviewed and assured by SLT.
- NQTs would receive regular formal and informal observation of teaching with immediate verbal feedback followed by written if a formal assessment.
- Follow up discussion and analysis with NQT by mentor and others if appropriate or requested.
- Assessments on NQT's teaching and progress against National Standards.
- Opportunities to observe other experienced teachers.
- A reduced timetable by 10 per cent.

As Forest School was also involved with the initial teacher training of student teachers if they subsequently became NQTs then the school linked those experiences with the induction year.

In practice the entitlement outlined above meant that during their induction to the school, NQTs met with key staff (to include the NQT mentor, Special Educational Needs coordinator and deputy head teacher) to discuss key polices. Career entry profiles were used initially to guide discussion between the mentor and NQT and therefore the direction of their development and training programme. Through this discussion a structured programme was developed which offered each NQT the opportunity to lead their training as supported by the NQT mentor. Targets (objectives) were set with a clear action plan of how they could be achieved, their link to teaching standards and the expected impact.

Meetings were held regularly to:

- Evaluate progress against action points,
- Evaluate progress against teaching standards,
- Reflect and review progress of individual NQTs,
- Set targets for further development.

Development included:

- Observations of staff (discussion included).
- Team teaching.
- Support in planning offered by subject/curriculum leaders.
- Support in the teaching of areas requiring specific skills such as PE (including swimming if appropriate) by external sports coach.
- Opportunities to observe in other schools; shadow subject/curriculum team leaders, work closely with subject/curriculum team leaders and lead on the development of areas/running of clubs.
- A structured programme was devised to support training and development.

Role as an external provider of initial teacher training

Forest School was in partnership with an initial teacher trainer and provided a base for the primary hub in the region. Support was given for the programme by offering training through workshops, team teaching, shadowing and discussion and if appropriate and providing placements for students. This was offered to create capacity in Forest School and to provide the school with a known group of students who could provide future NQTs. This also extended to providing places as part of the Graduate Teacher Programme.

Budgeting for development

The strategy of high quality and extensive CPD offered to staff at all leadership levels was a considerable expense to the school. The plan each year was carefully budgeted to ensure economies of scale. Included in this was an assessment of how the school could structure CPD opportunities which were effective, ensured a fair entitlement for all staff while still delivering value for money.

The factors determining success

Why did Forest School concentrate on ensuring effective staff development? The answer is twofold.

1   There was a belief in the principle that learning professionally should be an entitlement for staff. It helped them to develop their skills and capacity in their roles and self-esteem and enabled them to become reflective practitioners. It also encouraged staff recruitment and retention levels as staff both wanted to apply to work at Forest and to stay as they appreciated the opportunities to develop.

2   It was seen as key to ensuring high standards for children through the use of a highly skilled, well-motivated staff at all levels. It was believed that it was necessary to ensure continual improvement and to do that we needed to invest in high-quality teaching.

The following principles underpinned the action taken

The most important is to have high expectations of staff and to remember the power of trust where the underlying belief in school was that all wanted the best for the children, and it was the role of the school leadership to provide ways of enabling staff to achieve it. The following were considered to be important principles which underpinned the professional learning of staff:

●   Training, coaching and other forms of professional development should be about the personal as well as professional growth of the individual. Those who participate should feel that they have 'moved on' and are inspired to increase their knowledge further or use the skills and understanding gained to impact favourably on their own practice. This may be in terms of their career aspirations or the priorities of the school.

●   For this to be achieved, identifying just what were the learning needs of each individual (as well as team or whole school) was clearly essential. This could be done in a variety of ways, including feedback from pupils.

●   All more formal training opportunities should be structured to have clear outcomes which are relevant both for the individual and/or the organization. It was considered frustrating to undergo any form of training where the outcome did not match the aim or the training could not be applied to real situations in school.

●   Professional learning should be viewed as an entitlement for all members of staff. Decisions regarding the allocation of resources for staff development should be transparent and seen to be fair and equitable. Different forms of professional development should be valued which can involve bespoke coaching and mentoring and does not have to mean 'going on a course'.

- Professional development is effective if it is delivered in an appropriate environment and seen to be valued by the school's leadership. Training should be led by experienced and professionally credible presenters or facilitators who have a deep understanding of the subject. Many colleagues – both at Forest and from conversations the writer has had with other headteachers – felt that 'bolting on' important learning at the end of the school day had limited value.

- The opportunity to work in collaboration with other colleagues was a valued form of professional learning. Networking both formally during face-to-face sessions on programmes as well as in informal groups was considered essential for development. Placements in other schools or 'acting up' in one's own school was considered highly developmental in terms of refining practice and encouraging people to want to try the next 'step up' to leadership.

- Change and opportunities can occur during the year. Therefore flexibility should be built into the training plan reviewing and amending it as part of the school's self-evaluation processes with impact reported to stakeholders.(Adapted from Robinson [2010])

The trust and accountability which is invested in this approach requires high-quality leadership skills and a deep understanding of the vision and ethos of the school and commitment from staff to be the best they can be. It is necessary to have the wisdom to choose the 'right' time for development and what would make the most effective learning. Transparency and honesty were essential so that when praise was given it was believed and valued. When difficult conversations took place they were focused and developmental.

A good system which focuses on the needs of the school and individuals should also have an understanding of the national agenda for change. It should be forward-looking and manage leadership succession by anticipating both the national and local school's needs to create learners and leaders at all levels. All in school are leaders and followers determined by the current context.

The future

Professional development and training is never ending because the needs of the school, the children and individual members of staff, are ever changing.

While aspects may be short term such as training for a specific policy or the gaining of a qualification the ways learning may be generated for improvement is continuous.

The school and educational policy does not stand still and cohorts of children are individual. Staffs and their development needs change and so therefore while training plans are necessary so too is the realization that the learning journey changes and continues.

Summary of Chapter Eight

This chapter has:

- described the context at Forest School which led to the development of a consistent and embedded approach to continuing professional learning,

- in particular it has concentrated on the various strategies used to ensure development for all professionals at all levels and all types of staff role in the school and

- finally it has reflected on the key principles underpinning the work and offered the generalizing principle that learning is a continuous process which benefits both the individual members of staff and the pupils in their care.

CHAPTER NINE

The post-compulsory college: Investigating teaching and learning

Derek Warren and Cathy Francis-Wright

Introduction

In the United Kingdom, the post-compulsory sector (generally post-16 years of age and including adult education) is called the further education (FE) sector. The sector covers a huge range of vocational education. Against a background of significant change, this chapter describes how one FE college developed an approach to continuous professional development (CPD) to improve the quality of teaching and learning across the organization. This chapter will:

- describe the context of the college and the background to the sector,
- consider the professional development framework,
- identify ways of promoting a culture of personal and professional development,
- describe the impact on individual staff and
- describe the outcomes on teaching and learning within the college.

The context

The changing landscape within which the further education sector in the United Kingdom operates – economic stringencies, mergers, federations, cross-sector provision through school partnerships, academy and Studio School sponsorship, labour market changes, revised funding methodologies – presents particular challenges in relation to the recruitment of suitably qualified staff, matching skill sets to an increasingly broad curriculum offer and identifying the in-service professional learning needs of staff delivering learning for students and carrying out assessments.

The importance of developing the skills of staff has long been a feature of the continuous improvement agenda in the sector. Staff development and appraisal schemes, policies on support for further study, provision for short industrial placements, general terms and conditions, negotiations are all permeated with references to professional development. The Institute for Learning – the professional association for delivery staff in the sector – requires an annual record of CPD as a requirement of membership. However, the complexity that characterizes the sector requires an approach to professional development that can identify an individual's professional needs, use modes of delivery that have real impact on the quality of teaching and learning and at the same time take account of the multiplicity of shifting organizational requirements. Finding such an approach has increasingly become the goal for managers who have to identify, plan and deliver professional learning opportunities.

A particular aspect in relation to those who teach and assess vocational qualifications in this type of institution, is the high percentage of staff recruited who hold higher level specialist vocational qualifications, have extensive industrial experience BUT have limited or no experience of delivering learning. In addition, such staff are also often required to develop expertise in a 'second subject', gain higher level qualifications to enable the delivery of higher education provision in partnership with local universities or acquire skills to enable them to deal with students with acute behavioural or social issues.

Many staff in the sector do hold teaching qualifications though these are specifically focused on further education or the lifelong learning sector with many staff completing their qualifications in service. (Indeed, acquiring a teaching qualification while in service is a professional learning priority for many staff who have been employed from working in industry or outside the public sector.) However, qualifications are only a part of the equation; all staff must act as ambassadors of effective learning to all students, both in their work role and personally, and a core principle for CPD is that training and development investment will be made according to the college's strategic needs and direction. For example, as colleges expand their involvement with institutions in the school sector, staff are increasingly finding that a large proportion of their timetable is occupied delivering vocational learning to students in the 14–16-year-old age group with whom they have no previous experience or training, and staff not directly delivering learning find that they are now interacting with students and using processes that are very different to what might be termed the 'traditional' further education cohort.

This chapter looks at the systems and practices in one further education institution whose geographic, demographic and economic setting means all of the above factors apply to some degree. It is involved in delivering learning across the secondary, tertiary and higher education sectors. It delivers learning within all fifteen subject sector areas.[1] It operates across two County Councils, three Borough Councils and a range of Local Enterprise Partnerships.

The college's staff development policy states that 'The responsibility for on-going professional development should be shared between the College and its staff, who should be empowered to take control of their own development, with support from managers and the College as a whole'. Therefore, this college adopted an approach to meet the challenges of planning professional learning that has two key aspects.

First, a framework for identifying individual skill sets which match the needs of the college, its teams and individual members of staff. This is used within the college to inform development of training plans for all members of staff at every level: non-teaching, teaching, managers and executives.

Secondly, and more specifically in relation to teaching staff, this framework assists in identifying an individual's specific training needs and the broader needs of the teams in which they work. In this way individual plans are used to inform specific areas of training and encourage the sharing of identified effective practice within teams.

A vital aspect of delivering and monitoring progress against these plans is the role of a specially designated team of staff known as 'Quality Performance Leaders'. These specially trained staff perform a range of duties related to quality assurance and improvement strategies. This includes observations of teaching and learning sessions but more significantly in relation to professional development they work with individual members of staff on developing training plans and assist them in accessing appropriate activities to improve performance. They are teachers who have a strong track record of achieving high grades in observations of their own teaching and learning delivery and have a requirement that their own professional learning involves keeping abreast of current thinking in relation to effective practice and current teaching standards and the requirements of OFSTED. The majority of their time therefore is devoted to quality assurance activities – although they all retain some class contact. (Staff

1 The curriculum offer in further education is identified and inspected within fifteen subject sector areas.

with whom they work often quote this as an important element of the Quality Performance Leaders' (QPLs') credibility and their ability to work in an empathetic way.) The QPL's role is crucial in the process of identifying, supporting, monitoring and assessing professional development of staff who deliver learning within the curriculum context.

In determining the effectiveness of this approach, a range of impact measures are considered including: student success rates, satisfaction levels reported in stakeholder feedback surveys (staff and student), individual case studies and manager's appraisal of performance. The indications from these measures is that the key principles of being clear about the skills required and focused individual action plans within a culture of trust and support can be effective in improving standards of teaching and learning.

The Organization

The college is a large general FE college. Its curriculum offer is broad encompassing alternative provision for 14–16-year-olds, full-time programmes for 16–18-year-olds and 19+-year-olds from Entry Level 1 to Level 3. (Significantly, over the past five years, the college has recruited an increasing number of students on Entry Level and Level 1 programmes [lower level than GCSE] as the employment opportunities for these school leavers have diminished.) There is a large Access to Higher Education offer and a range of HNC/D (Higher National Certificate/Diploma) and degree programmes. In addition, the college delivers work-based learning and management training within industry. These programmes are delivered within all the subject sector areas. It has extensive and well-founded partnerships with local schools and following the closure of a Pupil Referral Unit in the area, the college has recently increased its alternative provision for 14–16-year-olds in the compulsory sector who were either excluded or at risk of exclusion. The college has two main campuses and a specialist centre for construction on the border between these two. It also has three outreach centres.

Corporate developments resulting in multi-site provision, cross-sectorial delivery, new demographic and socioeconomic factors in the recruitment profile have consequences for the professional development needs of staff as the character and range of teaching they deliver changes.

In total, the college employs 620 staff. Of these 250 plan and deliver learning or carry out assessment of learning. Of these, the staff hold or are currently working towards a recognized teaching qualification. The college delivers teaching qualifications to its own and other staff through a partnership arrangement with a local university.

The commitment to ensuring the highest standards of learning and teaching is outlined in the college's Aims and Values statement: 'To constantly improve the student experience', 'To trust and support each other', 'To ensure students achieve outstanding success rates'.

At the college's last OFSTED inspection in March 2012 it was graded '2 – Good' overall with Leadership and Management graded '1 – Outstanding'. Since then the college has improved its success rates and focused on further improving teaching and learning. The approach to CPD outlined in this chapter has, we believe, contributed to this progress. The further application and review of this process should enable the college to be nimble in its reaction to future challenges and ensure that it makes the most of the staff it appoints and provides them with the opportunity to review, update and develop their skill sets. Investors in People (IIP) has been continuously re-accredited at the college since 1995. Its federation partner college has recently been accredited with IIP Gold Status.

According to Lightbody (2012: 49), the best schools and colleges reduce the 'gamble' of the 'quality of teaching and learning they provide . . . through regular team talk, dissemination of good practice and observation schemes to drive the adoption and maintenance of commonly agreed standards often summarised within an agreed teaching and learning policy'.

The culture of shared values, clearly defined and matched skill sets to roles together with highly individualized planning and support for staff, we believe can produce a real impact on the standards of teaching and learning by ensuring that staff are equipped to teach effectively regardless of the issues which arise within the dynamic and fluid context of further education.

The professional development framework

The college has introduced its professional development framework with a view to ensuring a more proactive approach that articulates generic headline training needs.

The college's professional development framework is the means by which staff skill sets are matched to employment roles. As part of its development, Human Resources staff undertook extensive background research which helped to further define the skills, competencies, attributes and behavioural characteristics, relevant to each type of role. At its first tier it is a simple framework consisting of:

- Core competencies – job descriptions identify these as the basic needs that are essential to a role.

- Wider competencies – desirable training elements as relevant to a role.

- Specific competencies – training elements appropriate to vocation / career family . . . within the following role profiles (see Figure 9.1):

FIGURE 9.1 *Professional development framework.*

Role profiles

General and specific role requirements whether leadership and management, academic or support:

Whereas a job description conveys specific skills, qualifications, abilities and personal attributes required for the role, the college's professional development framework identifies detailed requirements pertinent to each role profile designed to give more focus and structure to the whole CPD process, ensuring consistency of approach. It is these competencies that now represent the core business requirements of the organization and present themselves in the form of a training matrix; one per profile category.

The ever-changing college profile, as outlined earlier in this chapter, provides particular challenges and opportunities to ensure that all staff develop their skills. Our vision has been to create a competency model which can be used to inform the identification of staff development needs, helping to identify training opportunities that can be facilitated for staff will positively impact on what might be termed the overarching 'organizational competence'.

'Essential' and 'Desirable' role requirements are identified within each job description, then collated, organized and displayed in matrix format to promote recognition. Consequently, this enables the college to better determine the requirements of all staff roles and provide a vehicle for structuring and planning personal and educational development and training on a cross-college basis.

Having established and prioritized bespoke training requirements, a wide range of staff from across a broad range of curriculum provision received a common programme of development activities and were given the opportunity to reflect upon improvements in practice.

An example that reflects the shift in skills requirements is training aimed at dealing with classroom management issues. This has become more prominent as the college recruits more Entry Level and Level 1 students – many of whom have poor behavioural records in school – and increases its work with 14–16-year-olds, particularly those students who have been, or are at risk of, being excluded from mainstream education. This shift has been challenging for many staff and the college has worked with the teaching unions to identify the professional training needs of staff to cope with this and inform the matrix. This competence has become more foregrounded and specific training was provided via external experts. An example of this is 'Promoting Positive Behaviour' training that was provided to staff involved in this area of work. This professional learning was accessed by both teaching and non-teaching staff. Feedback from staff who attended these sessions has been outstanding:

> 'Absolutely brilliant – Broadened my knowledge and made me re-evaluate the way I assist students.'

> 'Very informative session that provided some really good techniques to help in my role.'

> 'Interesting and enjoyable, I feel this has really helped me. I came into the session without much expectation that it would greatly increase my knowledge, but it definitely has.'

Teacher competencies devised as part of the overarching professional standards for teachers, tutors and trainers in this sector, were defined as part of the framework to supply the basis for the development of contextualized role specifications. These provide the benchmarks for performance in practice of the variety of associated roles. Together, they identified the components of the initial, intermediate and advanced training stages available to staff.

Promoting a culture of personal and professional development

In line with an initiative around cultural change facilitated by The Pacific Institute 'Investment in Excellence' programme which involves all college staff, the college continues to promote self-awareness and the development of one's self and others. The development and launch of the new CPD framework (2013–14) 'The Professional Development Framework' is a reflection of this.

Corporate themes within the college revolve around shared values and are enterprise-focused. Therefore, the professional development framework model promotes organizational 'Elements' (see Figure 9.2), which are the surface level of the structure:

FIGURE 9.2 *Corporate themes.*

It will also give more focus and structure to our whole appraisal process. How it all fits together (see Figure 9.3):

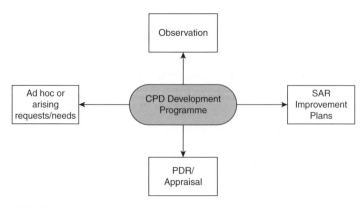

FIGURE 9.3 *CPD framework.*

Individual focus

The example quoted above relating to the provision of bespoke training – identified through the template – on managing and affecting student behaviour is typical of challenges that staff identify through appraisal, self-assessment plans, observation or meetings with managers. It is an example of a professional development need that runs across curriculum teams and where delivery to groups of staff can produce guidance which can be beneficial to staff immediately, but it can also lead to further training and support.

At the crux of providing such guidance and support on this topic and other identified individual needs are the college's QPLs. The individuals who make up this team are all teachers from various vocational sector backgrounds from across the college. They are attached to particular curriculum teams and work with managers and individuals on personal development plans. They provide a link between the individual and those internal and external agencies that might be able to assist in developing particular skills. More significantly, they assist staff in drawing up individualized action plans that can provide a focus on particular skills or identified needs that have arisen through observation, appraisal and discussion with managers in relation to the college's requirements. Each QPL has a caseload of teachers and/or assessors. This enables them to form strong relationships with the individual members of staff, their team leaders and their curriculum directors. They have the ability to coach and support others and to engage in and arrange for staff regular peer support.

We believe that this connection between the individual staff member and their managers has played a crucial part in improving the quality of teaching and learning. Staff feel that they can be open with their QPL about their professional development needs and managers have a confidential ear with whom they can discuss their perceptions of performance and agree improvement strategies and monitoring procedures.

For example, one curriculum director, who has seen significant improvements in success rates, teaching observation grades, stakeholder satisfaction feedback and awarding body quality-assurance feedback, gives credit to the impact of the work their QPL has done:

> In terms of moving things forward by working with individual members of our Directorate, the work of the Quality Performance Leader has been invaluable. She is someone who staff respect and accept that her agenda is about supporting them to improve their skills. In appraisals, staff recognize how the individual assistance they receive from the QPL has assisted them in practice.

This 'critical friend' aspect of the QPL's role and their ability to focus on individual need and broker appropriate support, both from within and without the college, is crucial to their success. The case studies that follow supports this perspective and reveal the impact that individual action planning and support of staff by the QPLs has on professional learning, particularly in relation to building confidence and overcoming the challenges that present themselves working in the modern further education milieu.

CASE STUDY 9A

DEVELOPING TEACHING SKILLS

Jane has been working at the college for around five years. Her vocational background is in the engineering industry. She has an impressive CV and, like many staff with extensive vocational knowledge and experience, was eager to use this in encouraging and equipping the next generation of engineers when she started teaching.

Her expectations – not uncommon in the sector – on embarking on her new career were that she would not necessarily require specific teacher training. She envisaged that her professional qualifications, work and life experience would equip her to teach students, whom she assumed would be highly motivated and ambitious to do well.

The reality she has faced has been very different. The extension of the range of programmes in this curriculum area – increased 14–16-year-old provision within the college and at partner institutions, more students below Level 2 (GCSE equivalent) and higher education students – has required Jane to develop specific approaches and strategies to teach across a diverse range of provision and provide for the individual learning needs of the students within it.

In particular, Jane has had to confront classroom management issues with students on lower level programmes and extend her planning skills in teaching those on higher level programmes.

In her appraisals, Jane's commitment to students and her willingness and desire to develop her teaching skills were noted. She identified areas that she felt she needed to improve: managing behaviour, planning theory sessions that could use more participation to engage students and sustain their focus. Also, as with all staff, she underwent her annual observation which recognized strengths in terms of her enthusiasm and high level of subject knowledge, but indicated the need to develop strategies in relation to the same aspects but particularly in relation to managing disruptive behaviour: Jane was often teaching classes that were entirely young men and whose individual learning profiles indicated that they had particular needs in relation to sustaining concentration and engagement with the subject.

Jane had already discussed aspects of her professional practice with her line manager and identified where her strengths lay and the areas she needed to improve. Using all these elements – appraisal, observation, one-to-one meetings, she worked with her designated QPL on developing an intensive programme of Teaching and

Learning Support. The areas for development focused on three key competencies:

- Managing behaviour
- Keeping students on track
- Pace of learning and assessment of learning.

The QPL was able to recommend a range of references and on-line resources for Jane to use between their scheduled review meetings. These included materials that had been used by an external educational consultant in professional development training particularly relating to practical ideas and resources for engaging students. Jane found these easy to access as the college has a bank of electronically stored resources in an area of its extranet. She said that they provided a good background to her work on specific learning sessions that she planned with the QPL, 'It might seem like an obvious thing, but when someone is working with you and is sharing their thoughts on the ideas contained in the College's resource bank, it's easier to consider them in terms of the work you are actually trying to plan.'

She was also referred to the college's Information Learning Technology (ILT) Staff Trainer/Developer. This meant that Jane was able to work on developing ILT resources that she had not considered previously as a means of varying activities within sessions and using audio–video resources more effectively. This included specific assistance in relation to developing competitive elements within teaching sessions through the use of quizzes, timed tasks and co-operative working approaches. The college has a national reputation in skills competitions and the development of resources to assist staff in incorporating competitive elements within teaching and learning sessions was something that has proved useful to staff such as Jane in considering ways to enliven sessions and motivate students.

She was also provided with a 'buddy' who was identified as someone who could demonstrate effective practice in relation to the three aspects and whose own teaching and learning sessions had been graded as 'outstanding'. This observation assisted Jane in identifying how some of the strategies she was working on could be effective in practice.

Progress against this plan was recorded in Jane's Teaching and Learning Support Log. This indicated where Jane was making progress and areas for further development.

The log records Jane's meetings with the QPL and her views on the effectiveness of the development activities on her practice. The log also records a number of support observations from the QPL that were the basis for further discussion and planning.

At the conclusion of the initial four-week period of support and development from the QPL, Jane had an observation from a different QPL to the one who had been supporting her and her grade had improved to '2 – GOOD' and specific reference in the observation report to the focused areas were all positive. For example, 'a variety of teaching strategies and activities including a practical demonstration, small group case studies and presentations to peer group. The teaching strategies successfully engaged all learners and the learners concentrated well teaching strategies successfully engaged all learners and the learners concentrated well and paid full attention,' and 'the pace of learning was good with no time wasted, the work was pitched at a level that was achievable for the group, they worked hard and tried their best. The learners confirmed that they felt that they were making sound progress and the teaching was helping them to achieve.'

Since then she has had external observations of her teaching and learning and her manager has informally observed her. Jane's response to the support and specific focus of the action plan was highly positive, 'I was well supported by the QPL throughout the period and this has continued since. There is no doubt that the one to one support has assisted me in making improvements to the way I plan my sessions. It has provided me with a broader tool-kit and given me more confidence.'

As part of her plan, Jane spent time with the QPL and her director on improving her planning to ensure better engagement of students. She also benefitted from peer observation which is something that the college is trying to develop more widely and in Jane's case was an important aspect of implementing some of the ideas she had developed.

Jane's profile is typical of many vocational staff in the sector; experienced practitioner, eager-to-develop skills, willing to engage in developmental activity, requirement to be flexible and teach students across several levels including students with behavioural issues. Having the opportunity to examine and develop an action plan for particular aspects of practice allied with college CPD events has proved positive in terms of her performance and her motivation to continue developing her teaching practice. Such a shift we consider, can only be driven by highly individualized personal development plans, one-to-one support, peer engagement within clearly identified organizational need.

CASE EXAMPLE 9B

IMPROVING INDIVIDUAL PRACTICE

Sabrina Butt is in her thirties. After obtaining a degree in International Political Studies, she worked in Business Administration. Four years later, she applied for a post teaching Information and Communications Technology (ICT) key skills part-time. She was appointed to the post and began delivering ICT to full- and part-time students of all ages and across all levels. While doing this she studied part-time and obtained the Post Graduate Certificate in Education (Further Education).

Owing to changes in Government policy key skills migrated into the wider functional skills programme. Subsequently the college's recruitment pattern resulted in more students requiring improvement in their literacy skills, and there was a requirement for more staff who could teach English. Consequently Sabrina was asked to add English to her timetable as well as ICT.

Accordingly, she took the opportunity to extend her own qualifications in line with the college's competency framework and supported by the college she completed the Level 5 Specialist Subject in Literacy.

Sabrina has a consistent record of grade '2 – GOOD' observations of her teaching sessions. A typical comment from an observation report is, 'A good degree of vocational knowledge was demonstrated when framing and answering questions. A range of student centred activities were used to tease out the students understanding.'

For this reason Sabrina's focus with her QPL has been on identifying aspects of practice that would enable her to improve her practice further and for her sessions to include more 'outstanding' elements.

To this end, Sabrina has attended sessions delivered by QPLs and tailored for those staff who regularly achieve grade 2s. She found this useful but like other members of staff feels that the individual support through one-to-one work with her designated QPL has had a real impact on her professional practice.

'Having the QPL to work with you on your plan makes it easier to find appropriate training and it's good to have the opportunity to 'pick up tips and think about practice' and they know who the best practitioners are and can put you in contact so you can see good practice in action. I feel I am more aware now of how I can refine some of my practice to provide that additional element that will make a difference.'

As with Jane the changing profile of the college's students has also been a challenge and a reason for her to focus on developing her skills to meet it:

> We have more students who enter programmes at Entry Level and Level 1 and more students in the 14–16 age range at the same time as having generally larger groups to teach.

This shift in Sabrina's personal timetable has meant she has attended external CPD sessions, but she feels the benefit of the support and review with her line manager and her QPL is the key factor in dealing with this change. The QPL has worked with her team and her as an individual on strategies for delivering to this age group and on developing resources and sharing best practice within college and with colleagues in partner institutions.

At her last observation Sabrina was again graded '2 – GOOD'. However, the report recognizes the outstanding elements in the lesson and she considers that the follow-up discussions with the QPL will enable her to continue on her personal journey of skills development and to achieving outstanding practice.

This, and being kept up to date on current OFSTED requirements and initiatives in relation to effective teaching and learning, are aspects that Sabrina recognizes as being a direct result of QPL activity.

Teaching functional skills, where finding new approaches to subjects that students feel they've already completed at school or on earlier programmes, is always challenging and is not helped by the ungraded nature of functional skills. Sabrina has, through CPD, been able to consider improving her practice by making more of her material vocationally relevant and introducing more varied tasks and challenges. Time she says is often restricted when you are working with students from across different vocational areas, but the QPLs help her make the most of the time available:

> Everyone has different needs and has different approaches to coping strategies. What works for one cannot work for all. Therefore, individual planning of CPD is essential in order to develop me as the best teacher I can be.

The attitude of Sabrina is one that is evident within the team in which she works. Following the work they have done individually with their QPLs they looked at how they could develop resources for other classes based on the effectiveness of what they had developed and learnt through their personal plans. This has led to the development of successful strategies and resources being stored in a 'shared area' that is available to all the team.

Although Sabrina's background and area of expertise are very different from Jane's, she too stresses the importance of relevance in the professional learning that the college facilitates.

She values the clarity of the stated skills related to her role and the ability to plan and discuss her needs with her QPL.

Improvement measures

In the last OFSTED report 2012 the quality of the college's observation process was noted:

The College has robust procedures for assessing the quality of lessons.

They noted particular aspects of impact of the development of individual teachers:

Managers use lesson observations well to identify development points for individual teachers as well as to highlight areas for development for the whole college. For example, incidences of lesson disruption have decreased following training for teachers in handling challenging behaviour.

Since then all the indications are that the college's approaches to improving the skills of those delivering learning and assessment continue to have an impact. It would be simplistic to attribute improved outcomes and more positive stakeholder feedback to the impact of a sharper and individualized approach to professional development. When scrutinizing the success rates across the college and within the individual curriculum areas there are many factors that impact on these. Nevertheless, it is interesting to note that the improvement in stakeholder feedback in relation to the quality of teaching and learning is contiguous with the improvement in success rates.

The overall college success rate in 2012/13 was 90.3 per cent. This has increased year on year and is 6.1 per cent above the National Benchmark for the Provider Group of 84.2 per cent.

Also, the success rates of qualifications studied by full-time students, (staff identify these programmes as those that often present significant challenges in successfully engaging students) have improved year on year over the past three years: 79 per cent in 2010/11 to 85.7 per cent in 2012/13 against a National Benchmark of 81.2 per cent. There has been a 3.4 per cent increase in long qualification success between 2011/12 and 2012/13.

Teaching and Learning	2011/12 Agree/completely agree %	2012/13 Agree/completely agree %
The teaching on my course is good	88	⬆92
Teachers use different ways to help me learn	86	⬆89
My sessions start on time	90	⬆91
My teachers treat us fairly and equally	82	⬆85
Assessment tasks are made clear to me	94	⬆95
Feedback tells me what I am doing well/need to improve	92	➡ 92

FIGURE 9.4 *Quality of teaching and learning.*

Similarly, for the 14–16-age cohort (this is the cohort that reflects the most marked shift in the timetables of staff) there is a three-year upward profile for achievement and success rates.

Figure 9.4 indicates the increased scores in stakeholder feedback in relation to some of the key questions related to the effectiveness of teaching and learning.

The college's last full IiP assessment identified as a priority that, 'learning and development activities for staff should be driven by the individual's desire to achieve rather than the essential skills for their role and the College should ensure these skills are being acquired'. We are convinced that the approach the college has taken in being clear and explicit about required skills sets and providing a mixed economy of cross-college and individualized professional learning programmes is the most effective way of meeting the challenges what might be called the new FE agenda and ensuring professional learning is driven by each member of staff's individual need.

Conclusion

The creation of the team of QPLs has had a strong impact on the quality of teaching and learning. The individual focus and support has been instrumental in enthusing staff and enabling them to access training and support that meets their needs. As economic pressures increase, the need to increase staff utilization will become more acute. The challenge will be to sustain what might be considered an expensive resource. However, if FE colleges are to meet the challenges of the ever changing context in which they operate, and provide the very best learning experiences for their students, they need to ensure that staff:

- feel valued
- can develop their professional skills and their achievements
- are celebrated
- receive appropriate remuneration.

Summary of Chapter Nine

This chapter has:

- described the FE sector and the context of the college,
- explored the professional development framework,
- identified ways of promoting personal and professional development for individual staff and
- summarized the impact on teaching and learning within the college.

CHAPTER TEN

The Abu Dhabi schools and researching staff needs in a centralized system

*Ayman Hefnawi, Auruna Rajah,
Uwem Umana with Philip Whitehead and
David Middlewood*

Introduction

This chapter explores the relatively new experience of providing continuous professional development (CPD) programs at public schools in the Emirate of Abu Dhabi, United Arab Emirates (UAE), and in the process influencing a shift in teachers' attitudes towards their personal and professional learning. The chapter therefore:

- describes the context for the study and the proposed changes,
- gives examples of how advisers and teachers set about implementing the changes,
- draws out some of the implications for the teachers involved in terms of their learning, and discusses some of the principles discerned,
- discusses the extent of generalizability of the issues from this context to wider ones and
- considers briefly some future possibilities for development.

Context

In the UAE, the leadership of the Emirate of Abu Dhabi identifies education as a high priority to attain a progressive society and to achieve its striving goal of becoming a leading knowledge economy (abudhabi, 2013). Accordingly, the government started a large-scale educational reform to elevate the quality of education in the emirate to international standards (abudhabi, 2013). The education reform started by establishing Abu Dhabi Education Council (ADEC) in 2005 in accordance with the presidential law of 2005 to be responsible for developing the education and the educational institutions in the emirate. In order to seek the intended development, ADEC adopted a variety of educational initiatives; one of these initiatives was the public private partnership (PPP) project that started in 2006. The project aimed at leveraging the expertise of private school operators (learning providers) to enhancing public schools operations through improving the quality of teaching. An ADEC priority was the provision of professional development programs for all teachers and school leaders in all of its schools. Thus, the learning providers designed and implemented these programs in the schools they worked in. It was a new experience for teachers to have these programs running inside their schools on a regular basis, as they formerly used to attend separate professional development sessions outside their schools for certain purposes, for example, a training to implement a new maths curriculum. This was done on a straightforward model, not uncommon in countries with a centralized educational system, that is, a new initiative is announced by the central authority, and this is passed down to the individual institutions and all staff are trained to deliver the new procedure. Often these include the use of one specified textbook in a subject.

This new reform was centred on moving teaching and learning away from an old-fashioned rote-learning system to a learner-centred one. Since, ultimately the aims of emiratization included employing more UAE citizens as teachers and thus relying less on foreign expatriates, the changes envisaged may be seen as preparing the next generation of teachers. These future 'home grown' teachers therefore needed to be able to facilitate the new kind of learning and, it could be argued, to be professional learners themselves. Clearly, within the limits of the new kind of professional development offered, the providers and the advisors had more individual scope than previously where the system for CPD had been as described above. As already indicated, initially, several advisors encountered resistance to the new approaches that some of them were keen to put in place.

The status of PD in the post-PPP era (since 2012)

By the 2012 school year the PPP project was ended in most of ADEC schools; ADEC decided to continue providing professional development programs for teachers and schools' leaders through a new project initiative called '*Tamkeen*', an Arabic word meaning *empowerment*, aims at supporting the development of qualified and skilled school leaders and teachers to enhance the quality of educational outcomes achieved by students (ADEC, 2013c). It is a large-scale training program; during the 2012/13 school years, the Tamkeen program served 248 schools, delivering a total of over 300,000 hours of training to school leaders and teachers in ADEC government schools (ADEC, 2013c). The training content material is designed mainly by ADEC in association with representatives of the learning providers, who originated from the United Kingdom, New Zealand, Canada and the United States. Further research is needed to examine the '*Tamkeen*' program that perceived impact on the schools' leaders and teachers. No claim is made in this chapter about the impact upon the nation's schools as a whole, but sufficient evidence exists through the experiences of the three advisors contributing here to indicate that it is possible to make considerable steps towards the eventual goal of a learner-based system; the key stage may well be that of teachers themselves becoming effective and committed learners. As Darling-Hammond (2006) noted, effective teachers are those that commit themselves to lifelong, or at least career-long, learning. As the rest of the chapter shows, the vast majority of the teachers responded to the developments led by the advisors in a way that shows what may be possible in the future. Each of the advisors having more autonomy than previously, they felt able to choose the professional learning approaches that they believed were most likely to be effective in the specific context.

What did these advisors have in common?

- Each had studied in Abu Dhabi for a Master's degree in education from Warwick University, tutored by a teaching fellow who had led sessions in Abu Dhabi for the group.

- Each therefore had a good knowledge of educational theory and also the practical professional experience to relate these to effective practice. They therefore had an understanding of adult learning theory and its relevance to teachers. Through this, they knew the importance of the specific context within which learning takes place.

- They all knew that discussion between teachers – especially in the new context – would be crucial in the success or otherwise of the new professional learning developments.

- They all knew the importance of CPD or professional learning in any form being linked to identified needs of those receiving CPD or developing their own learning, because in that way the learning would be meaningful and relevant to them individually.

- Finally, and very importantly, they were well aware that all such professional learning had to ultimately lead to a positive impact on pupil learning to be shown in pupil attainment.

- This meant that careful evaluation of any CPD and/or professional learning was critical and any such evaluation also needed to be related to pupil learning.

If we examine three examples of how the professional learning was developed in different ways, it may be possible to give an indication of future possibilities.

The first example (A) was in a girls' school for Grades 6–9, located about 30 kilometres outside the city centre in a developing suburb. The advisor initially met such strong resistance to any kind of CPD and change that she requested a transfer. However, after inspections and pressure on the school to improve attainment, there was a realization of the value of some kind of training or development and the advisor was asked to return to the school, a request now supported by several staff. The advisor realized that whatever was put in place, it had to have a foundation which would last after she had left at some point in the future. Therefore, any strategy needed to be rooted in real learning on the part of the teachers.

The first step was to get the teachers to identify what their specific learning needs were, in terms of what was most beneficial to the pupils. The school was committed to a 'No child left behind' approach and the Maths Action plan had to be seen in the light of this whole school approach, stated in the School Improvement Plan. After discussion and analysis of their feedback to each other, the teachers concluded that while lower ability pupils had been well supported, the higher ability ones had little done for them to stretch and fully use their abilities. In some cases, these were highly gifted and talented children. The teachers then identified that extension activities beyond the classroom were needed to support these particular pupils and, interestingly, it was the single newly qualified teacher (NQT) on the staff who made the suggestion of a 'Maths Challenge'. This would take the form of a competition where classes would enter a team of four to attempt 'creative and critical thinking' questions – in the medium of English. With the support of the Head of Maths, this was agreed and at this point, the advisor took the opportunity to introduce the teachers to a kind of action research approach for the implementation of the challenge. Not only did she think it would facilitate the project, but that it could also offer teachers a tool for future use in developing their own learning in any approach to new initiatives.

Following the standard format, they had first identified the problem, and next had to draft a plan. The possible different formats for the challenge were discussed and debated in depth. Eventually, the plan was for a class team competition and teachers were now involved in writing questions for the competition and methods for collecting data and ultimately evaluating the success of the project. Following the general guidance of Middlewood and Abbott (2012), a survey approach using questionnaires for both the pupils and the teachers was adopted. A creative approach was felt by the advisor to be necessary because of the tentative attitude of teacher participants towards research. They had also not been accustomed to reflection on their practice. The survey tool therefore took the form of a questionnaire with a speech bubble that required teachers to express two stars (the positives) and a wish (how they would like to improve on the competition).There was no restriction on how many stars or wishes they could include. The pupil questionnaires were simple translated surveys using the Likert scale. Visual aids were used as descriptors of the Likert scale responses to assist pupils in understanding the alternative responses available.

In effect the actual Maths Challenge was the 'intervention' in the action research. It took place and the overall responses were very encouraging with more than 90 percent of students stating high enjoyment and more than three quarters of them asking for even more challenging questions next time! Over ninety percent felt that their enthusiasm for Maths had increased.

As far as reflection was concerned, the words in the speech bubbles proved very helpful. Via this reflection, the advisor found that the teachers had not only been able to identify the positives in their experiences, but to also think about what changes they would like to see and, significantly, how these changes could be brought about through their own practice development. In effect, these teachers were examining their own practice and now identifying ways of moving forward, thus taking ownership of their own learning and development.

> If I have a development in mind for improvement, and I am not sure how to bring that about, I know it is not a weakness to admit I do not know, because all of us have some weaknesses, and by sharing and discussion, we can offer suggestions and find a way forward for me. (Teacher A)

Significantly, this teacher went on to comment that 'this way forward will work for me, I hope, but for someone else, it may not be the best. We can all help each other, and find the best way for each person. As long as the pupils get the best deal, in the end that is of course what matters.'

The advisor felt strongly that the concept of the wish had been powerful in enabling people to acknowledge that some aspects had not gone well and that changes needed to be made. Reflective practice as a learning tool, she felt, while an accepted element of Western practices, was not normally something many teachers were conscious of in developing countries, although possibilities were emerging (see Ashraf and Rarieya, 2008). The reflective dialogue used earlier in identifying the need to cater for highly able pupils was now helping to facilitate teachers' later thinking about future development. As an indication of the increased confidence in their own professional learning, the advisor invited two of the Maths teachers to present at a 2011 Lead Practitioner Conference with a session titled 'Maths the Emirates Way'. Although very nervous, the contributors' success was evidenced by the feedback which, among other things, showed that seven other schools planned to hold their own Maths challenges. The teachers in the school described here were adamant that they themselves would hold another next year, regardless of whether the advisor support was there or not! In reflecting on the whole experience, the advisor believed that the teachers in future would be clear that all forms of CPD would have to meet their own needs and that constant refection, particularly collectively, would not be something they would give up. She also was clear that, as here in terms of impact on Maths learning, they were clear that all their professional learning had to be linked to growth in their pupils' learning and progress.

The second example (B) comes from an all-boys' school in Abu Dhabi where the English Advisor had been asked to work with licensed teachers (LTs) to help improve their development as classroom teachers. These teachers had been very critical of the established way of their receiving any kind of professional development, as already described. They had made it clear that they felt such 'training' had not been relevant to their individual professional needs. He felt therefore that the priority was to enable this needs identification to occur. With another assisting advisor, he decided to use reflective journals and diaries as the research method to discover the extent to which, over a period of time, ideas about their practice and related developmental needs could develop. The two advisors themselves kept journals and/diaries so that some form of triangulation could exist. The value of this research tool lies in its ability to reflect thoughts and emotions of those involved. A small number of the LTs volunteered as the research group. Whether reflective practice of this kind could be effective was a kind of act of faith at this stage (Russell, 2005).

Analysis of the entries in the diaries and journals, examining both content and language, showed a significant development in the thinking of the LTs about their learning and practice. A small selection of these entries gives a flavour of this development.

At the beginning, a recurring negativity is clear in the LTs' entries with regularly used phrases such as: 'a waste of time', 'not beneficial to me' and 'done because it had to be done'. One of the advisors noted how his offer of help with resources was rejected with 'I don't need them'.

By the middle of the year, comments include ones that discussions where the LT has then gone away to reflect are 'more beneficial' and 'professionally helpful'. They note that post-lesson critiques where the advisor asks questions and the LT thinks out his own answer are proving valuable because the LT is thinking for himself. For example:

- Why did you do that?
- Did you get the result you wanted?
- Was there something different you could have done? And so on.

The later entries show such discussions being referred to as 'engaging in a process of honestly evaluating what went well, what could be changed and how'. One entry notes that 'my personal strengths are now being utilised'.

Also, the value of the LTs sharing ideas between themselves, independently of the advisors, is strongly evidenced in the later entries. A notable change in language in the LT later entries is the use of 'we' instead of 'I', as in the early ones.

> As we gained knowledge of our students and learned more about teaching them, our reflections often focused on how we felt limited in being able to help each and every student function at his highest level. In these reflections, we managed to forgive ourselves and each other for not being able to do everything when students have so many needs. In turn, this led to us reflecting on how we could work together for the good of all students. My point is that these reflection sessions were not merely times to share ideas, although that is important; they led to strategic thinking on how each of us could work from our strengths while we are all actively supporting our students.

Here is evidence of the foundations of a professional learning culture being laid, where teachers are not just interested in the particular class in front of them but in all the classes, and the understanding that shared professional learning benefits them as individual practitioners, and all colleagues and all students as well. In this context, it was interesting to note entries which welcomed 'expert' resources offered by advisors, because personal pride was no longer at stake, as earlier, but the sources were merely another helpful way to improve practice and thereby student learning.

It is important not to suggest this all happened smoothly! Reference is made to 'many disagreements, sometimes vehement in nature and tone', to 'disagreeable moments', but the realization about learning through failure is evident.

> The myriad challenges of teaching the students here almost requires that one fails at times, for failures in teaching, as in many aspects of life, often carry and hold the key to later successes – if there is honest reflection to help one learn from one's mistakes and shortcomings.

What this advisor believed was that the whole approach was very positive because no one pedagogy was imposed on another person, that the atmosphere of 'trust and honesty' and being 'non-threatening' was crucial, and that stepping outside of the role of expert into one of co-learner had been the keys. We need to note of course that the learning experience here for the advisors themselves had been significant, something to be taken forward into new experiences, where the learning gained here would be used.

Clearly, another important aspect of teachers' professional learning is that the most recent learning experience, whatever form it takes, should be carefully evaluated so that improvements may be made in any future learning or learning provision.

The third example, (C), from Abu Dhabi is from an all-boys' school there with a teaching staff of nearly thirty, and a Maths advisor/provider who had been there for about five years. It involved a controlled piece of research into the evaluation by a sample of eight teachers of the CPD provision of the previous year. The eight were in two groups, one teaching in Arabic and one in English; the former had no close links with the advisor, whereas the second group of four did. Because the investigation through the evaluation was focused on the professional identities of the teachers, the second group were keen to participate and address the questions:

- How did they perceive the way the CPD influenced their practice?

- To what extent were their personal professional needs met through the provision?

- How useful was the evaluation in moving forward their own future professional learning?

In addition to the normal evaluation sheets completed during the programme after each session, semi-structured interviews were carried out with four individuals and the school principal, as well as focus group interviews with each of the two groups (see Middlewood and Abbott, 2012).

The findings showed that the programme offered affected teachers' classroom practice where practical activities and specific skills were able to be directly applied from the sessions to the classrooms. Sessions which were seen as more theoretical were seen as unhelpful and impact on practice as very limited. The development of these classroom skills led to improved student behaviour, better attitudes to learning and even improved punctuality at lessons. The actual provision of the programme led to teachers having discussions about teaching and learning and through those it was felt that an improved learning environment had developed.

The group that worked more closely with the advisor had more scope to try out new teaching approaches and new strategies such as co-teaching, mutual observation and subject departmental workshops.

The teachers' individual professional needs had by and large not been met by the provision, except where specific teaching skills had been offered. Even in those cases, it was to some extent a matter of chance whether an individual person's needs had been met through what had been on offer. Those who had worked more closely with the advisor had more chance of having their needs met than the others.

On the evaluation question, it was strongly felt that as the evaluation stood at present, it was largely ineffective because of its focus on participant satisfaction and hardly at all on impact.

The conclusions from this small study in this particular context were that:

- The role played by the school leader could be significant if the principal would have post-CPD discussions to discuss learning outcomes with individuals, ideally carry out observations before and after the CPD, and contribute to suggestions for future professional learning base on these.

- Provision of a general CPD programme was of hugely limited value unless effort was made to address the individual or small team needs. It was crucial that these be included in the planning for any future provision.

- Any parts of the provision which involved theoretical considerations needed to be linked closely with practical aspects showing how theory might be translated into practice, or at least investigated in a practical way.

- Future evaluations of future programmes should occur after a period of time, when there has been an opportunity for impact to be assessed and for reflection on its value.

- Finally, apart from any formally structured provision, opportunities should be sought for teachers to have discussions, both at subject level, and collectively, to facilitate informal professional learning.

Possible implications for the national education system concerned

The three advisors concerned were all clear that in no way could their own very specific case studies be taken as any kind of blueprint for all schools in Abu Dhabi or the Emirates at large. Each piece of work was specific to its own school context and indeed the three schools did not work together in any sense. Nevertheless, it is interesting to consider what implications there are in the studies, what principles that they have in common can be discerned and whether there are possibilities for development on a wider scale.

Common features and principles summarized:

- The first and very obvious is that teachers' professional learning needs to be recognized as having ultimately one key purpose, namely the improvement of the pupils' or students' learning. Obvious though this is, it cannot be stated too often, and, in a context such as this where there is considerable emphasis placed on international comparisons and therefore a need to raise national standards to bring the nation on a par with others, it can never be neglected. Of course, the same is true of all developed countries in today's global context.

- The importance of ensuring that any form of professional development or professional learning has at its core the recognition that it should attempt to meet the professional needs of the recipients, so that they can understand its relevance to them and their practice. Given that all the cases found considerable dissatisfaction with the normal model of 'one size fits all' CPD on the grounds of its irrelevance to individual teachers and therefore to the detriment of their own pupils, this meeting of personal professional needs is paramount.

For this to happen, there has to be some form of needs identification taking place at various levels, not just national. Ideally, this should include school level, subject department level and individual level. This needs identification can take various forms, but should be in a structured way.

- There should be opportunities for teachers to reflect on their practice, on any changes that have occurred, and on the effectiveness or otherwise of such changes. This means time, possibly structured time, where this can happen and be encouraged.

- Discussions between teachers and the chance to collectively debate issues of theory and practice are of crucial importance. Not only do these prove valuable to individuals but over time they inevitably foster an environment or culture which facilitates learning development at an informal level and which research shows to be of great significance in professional learning.

- The way the role of the specialist expert is developed is important; it is most effective when it is operated not as a top-down model, but one within an environment which enables teachers to seek help as discerned by internal debate, although such changes cannot happen overnight.

- Any evaluation of provision of professional learning needs to be carried out in a way which takes into account its impact on practice and which can then be fed into planning for future provision.

- The role of school leaders can be crucial in developing and supporting all the above.

All these underline for the three advisors that effective professional learning has the potential to be improved dramatically for the benefit of teachers and thereby of pupils. However, in any system where there is national pressure to conform, progress towards even relative autonomy for individual institutions may be difficult. Since the topic at issue here is the development of teachers, it is not appropriate to speculate on the way the education system as a whole operates. It can be argued that even in a system where there is a common curriculum and common attainment is being striven for, the accountability can still be operated at the institutional level. In other words, where the end result is effective, the exact way in which an individual school achieves this can be left to the school leader, as long as national values are respected and appropriate procedures are followed. Certainly, at least one of the given examples suggested that an increased role for the school leader could be significant.

In terms of professional development, the argument would be that if the school is effective in developing its teachers in a way that enhances pupil learning and attainment, it would be hard to argue with its operation. The wider significance in the emirate is the publicly stated aim to make the education system less reliant on foreign staff and produce more native teachers. The signs here would be encouraging if the way in which many teachers responded in the three given examples and were able to demonstrate understanding of increased professional learning which had an individual identity aspect to it were typical of teachers in general. This is because, just as the examples showed promising signs of a professional learning culture developing within individual schools, there would be a likelihood of such cultures spreading across schools. Movement and perhaps even the training of the advisors could be relevant here, as could the mobility of actual teaching staff. Ideally, a profession of teachers who saw themselves as professional learners could have a major impact on the learning and attainment of the nation's pupils and future citizens. However, this has to be speculation, and many barriers lie in wait, since education, as in all countries, cannot be separated from societal, political and religious issues which affect the situation to a huge degree. One could mention also the language issue, common to many countries where there is a wish to teach all children in both their native tongue and also an international language – of which English is the major example at present. It is noted that in one of the cases studied that the Arabic-only speaking staff were more reluctant than the English-speaking staff to embrace new approaches and again it is not difficult to speculate as to why this could be so, without passing judgement, or to know how far this is any kind of indication as to how widespread such an issue is. Considerably more research would need to be undertaken to explore such areas as these.

Of course, any implications for the UAE as a whole are impossible to be clear about, since, as Thorne (2011) noted, four of the ten emirates have in effect abandoned the state system in favour of private alternatives. The fundamental tension between the widely recognized need for change and the conservative nature of the UAE education system means that great obstacles exist to the likelihood of some of the above becoming widespread. Whether the 'moral purpose' that Thorne (2011: 181) sees as essential 'to challenge the prescriptions of mandated change' is there on a wide scale is unknown, although it is clearly evident in specific individuals and schools. What IS clear is that professional development will have a vital role to play and improving that development and professional learning is a key ingredient in successful change.

Is there generalizability from these cases to other education systems?

To what extent can the cases described here in Abu Dhabi have any significance for professional development in other countries and thereby for pupil attainment?

First, one can consider if there are implications for those countries which tend to operate an education which is centralized, as opposed to those which operate autonomous or semi-autonomous systems. Even here, already a large range of types exist, from heavily centralized and controlled, to ones primarily centrally controlled but with some regional autonomy, from those with reliance on set textbooks administered from the centre to those where a national curriculum is established but resources left to local authorities. There is also a distinction to be made between developed and developing countries, where the huge differences in resources allocation does not at all reflect the differences that may exist between types of systems as described.

Even if countries or states are seen to be similar in certain ways, it is important here to note the reservations and potential pitfalls lying in wait for those who wish to transpose one successful system into another place for the purpose of improvement. While at individual institutional level, this might work in some contexts, so often it is politicians at national level who may fall prey to this notion of a relatively speedy solution to 'home' problems. To take one example, in the second decade of this century, Finland has rightly been lauded for its huge success in school and pupil achievements, as shown in PISA international tables.

However, most researchers, including Finnish ones, have warned of the unlikelihood of success in merely imitating Finnish procedures. Sahlberg (2011) warns that the Finnish model cannot be simply copied, or indeed that picking up one component for transfer is not likely to work because all components are integrated in one whole. Further, educational, political and cultural factors specific to Finland play a huge part in the schools' success and were developed over time (Antikanen, 2006). These may be greatly different from a society which hopes to import the system. Teaching being highly esteemed in Finland and it being a relatively homogeneous society (OECD, 2013) are just two of various factors which contribute to its success and are not at all applicable in some countries hoping to use its system. The Finnish example here is simply one which illustrates the risks (of failure) in seeing success elsewhere and believing that the use of the successful system in the home nation will bring equal success. A study of government initiatives over a period of years, for example in England, reveals how different ministers have enthusiastically recommended practices which work effectively in their own contexts (1990s Pacific Rim nations, for example) but which have tended to disappear eventually after some experimentation in the country. Education is so intrinsically part of a country's history and culture that it is unlikely to succeed without those factors being taken account of.

In the twenty-first century with its inevitable stress on globalization, all countries face significant barriers to raising achievement but research has indicated that those in situations similar to UAE face ones such as:

- 'Traditional thinking' (Alsaeedi and Male, 2013: 655) re Kuwait
- 'Strong cultural values' (Yin et al., 2014: 306) re China
- 'Directive forms of leadership' (Mottar, 2012: 508) re Lebanon.

The biggest feature, that is, 'Most notably the central decision-making taken by the Ministry of Education' (Alaseedi and Male, 2013: 654) leads to the current potential tension in various countries' education systems between this decision-making from the centre versus scope for development at regional level. Additionally, the scope for an individual institution being able to experiment with a single component from a successful overseas model is not likely to be permitted.

School and college leaders serve local communities and therefore cannot evade their local cultural and social contexts. Above all, the teachers being key to raising pupil achievement, their continuing development is crucial. Here, the actual allocation of staff to schools from the centre without consideration of local issues can be an inhibiting factor on both the teachers' willingness to develop themselves through professional learning (see Middlewood, 2001 re Greece; Simeon, 2009, re Seychelles) and the principal's ability to motivate them (see Thorne, 2011, re UAE).

Nevertheless, one virtually universal factor in all studies examining these dilemmas is the realization and recommendation, relevant to the theme of this book, is the emphasis on the need for the professional learning of teachers. As Katzenmeyer and Moller (2011) noted, the raising of teachers' self-esteem and work satisfaction through professional development is almost certain to lead to enhanced performance and enhanced pupil learning and attainment. In turn, this will increase the chance of teacher leadership flourishing in such settings (Mottar, 2012) and thereby encouraging local decision-making.

Furthermore, there is agreed emphasis that such learning must address the specific needs of the teachers in their specific contexts. Since all the studies also call for further research or a definite 'research base' (Thorne, 2011:182), we would argue that such needs identification may well be best attained by the kind of professional in-house inquiry that much of this book is concerned with. The three cases in Abu Dhabi described earlier in this chapter, while in no way offering any kind of simple solution, may on the other hand offer helpful examples of how such profession learning, linked with in-house research, can give inspiration for those seeking change. As Yin et al. (2014) suggested in China, a far larger scale case study than most others, there is likely to be scope for what they call a 'workable compromise' (ibid.: 308) and the effectiveness of such small-scale studies can perhaps help in 'transforming contradictions into learning opportunities and even using dilemmas as a positive leverage for change' (ibid.: 309).

Summary of Chapter Ten

This chapter has been concerned with professional learning, often delivered through conventional CPD programmes in schools in Abu Dhabi. It has:

- described the context of the education system in Abu Dhabi,

- given three examples of advisors working with teachers to facilitate new forms of professional learning,

- tried to elicit implications and principles from those examples for the education system concerned,

- discussed possible issues that may be relevant in other contexts and discussed the ones involved in 'borrowing' from other countries and

- discussed briefly possibilities of relevant future developments.

PART THREE

Overview

CHAPTER ELEVEN

Conclusions and reflections

Introduction

In this final chapter, we reflect on any implications emerging from the previous ones and discuss whether there are any conclusions that can be drawn from them, as well as considering what future possibilities exist in the world of professional learning and its impact in education. This chapter therefore:

- summarizes briefly some of the significance of the practices and principles related to professional learning presented earlier,

- attempts to draw out a few conclusions arising from them,

- reflects on the nature of these conclusions and their potential applicability to future work and

- briefly considers some possibilities for the future of professional learning.

Significance of professional learning

Research across most of today's world has indicated very clearly that the two biggest factors in improvement in educational standards are the quality of teaching and learning, and the quality of leadership and management (Robinson, 2007; Leithwood et al., 2010). The continuous improvement of teachers through professional development and learning therefore is and will remain of the greatest importance in all countries and all educational institutions, whether schools, colleges or universities. We are convinced that the effectiveness of teachers, lecturers, leaders and managers is part and parcel of their personal identities, attitudes and philosophies and that therefore their development is best considered as professional learning. Along with many others, we have argued that the key to this effective development is enabling it, in whatever form it takes, to be relevant to the needs of those concerned and to be perceived by them as being relevant. Although needs identification can take various forms, we have argued that one of the most effective and powerful is through carrying out internal structured investigation, done by the teachers and lecturers themselves and also by the learners, that is pupils and students. As stated regularly, for this to work, the actual in-house inquiry must be of high quality and of a professional standard.

The numerous examples given in the book, some of them in considerable detail, have shown how the learning and development of those involved, whatever the type of educational institution, can benefit hugely from this process. This of course includes the pupils and students themselves, which is the ultimate point of improved professional learning. As with any respected profession, the ability to strive constantly for improvement in one's practice lies at the heart of the most effective practitioners in every context. In the hurly burly of everyday working life, finding time to reflect on one's practice and how it might be developed is one of the most difficult things and this is possibly why 'going on a course' was for so long the apparently easy way to learn something new. Someone else perhaps had the answers! The realization that often the best way forward lay near at hand – in one's own place of work, or in a nearby own – was slow to develop, but it is now widely recognized that learning in context is most likely to be effective. When one's friends and colleagues, and even one's students, are part of this learning, the impact is even more powerful.

What conclusions may be drawn?

One of the obvious conclusions is that some form of research or inquiry is central to the proper development of educational professionals. When it is seen as relevant, is in the work context, and its dissemination is managed as we have described, it generates new professional knowledge and awareness and will become an extremely powerful agent for effective change. As we have seen, when this research becomes embedded in the normal work of a school or college, effective change is not seen as a threat, but as something to be desired because it is based on the reality of the professionals' own developmental needs. These themselves are for the benefit of the institution's core customers – the pupils or students.

Another conclusion is that professional learning can take many forms and can also be unexpected in the way that opportunities for learning can arise. While structured opportunities will continue to be needed, the professional learning culture as we have described shows that such opportunities will be spotted and taken up by those learners who see a chance to improve even more. As in life itself, learning occurs in all kinds of unexpected ways and situations, and the committed professional grasps these opportunities readily.

A crucial point that has arisen is that, while individual development is essential, most professional learning will occur most effectively in a shared context. While only one chapter has been specifically entitled as being about collaborative practice, in reality, the vast majority of examples have involved sharing with others in one way or another, sometimes with peers, sometimes with those in other roles, sometimes a teacher–pupil partnership. In a future which looks as if, at least in a large number of countries, it will involve more combining of schools, partnerships and networks, such sharing will be of crucial importance. In an increasingly fragmented education system, such as in England and Wales, or the United States, the need for consistency of effective practice in the interests of learners becomes even more important. Therefore, teachers, in whatever form of school they work, can benefit from what is often called now 'joint practice development' or JPD (Sebba et al., 2012).

Another conclusion is surely that whole schools and colleges can be transformed through the development of a culture of professional learning. Achieving this is not a quick or easy process, but as some of our examples have shown, it can be done. It should be stressed that this is not at the expense of attainment in the measurable ways so often demanded by national governments. Far from it – as examples clearly show – schools and colleges with this culture achieve highly in examination and test results and at the same time encourage their learners to understand and enjoy learning, something they can continue to do throughout adult life as future citizens.

Arendt (1993) has likened any form of research or inquiry as an essential way of illuminating in difficult or dark times. This is because, we believe, in-house inquiry can 'dig' beneath the surface of political or popular rhetoric and find the reality on which effective learning can be built. Whichever image you prefer, the 'flickering light' of Arendt (ibid.: ix) or the diving for pearls of Gunter, Hall and Mills (2014), the conclusion is the same, that through carefully structured and committed inquiry can real improvement be founded.

What are the implications for future practice?

One of the most important implications is that any definition of an effective school or college in the future would include its ability to have a focus on internal inquiry. Regardless of the precise term ('research engaged', 'research based', 'research involved' or whatever), there will be a clear understanding that only a school or college that is capable of showing that it can pursue its own improvement through internal inquiry can be properly seen as a truly effective institution. Such a capability therefore would become one of the key criteria for any external inspection process. For institutions that were seen as too small for this to be feasible, such a criterion would apply across the group, family or chain of which it is part, with each school being assessed within that framework.

Equally, when new initiatives are proposed at national levels, these are made easier to implement with full understanding which can best come about through research by the practitioners affected. For example, in a report by the National College for Teaching and Leadership in England, the authors recommended that new assessment procedures involved a 'culture shift' (Lilly et al., 2014: 38) and that teachers needed to be 'research-active' (ibid.) so that technical changes could be underpinned by 'professional learning about the range and purposes of assessment' (ibid.).

A second implication will be that the debate about professionalism in education will be affected. This debate about whether teaching is or can be a profession in the same or even different way that others such as law or medicine are has existed for some time. Whether the notion of professionalism is seen as 'idealistic' (Hoyle, 1995: 69) or a matter of context (Ozga, 1995), the model of teaching as shown in this book affects this notion. In the modern context of self-managing institutions such as in Australia, (Knight et al., 1994) and in New Zealand (Gordon, 1992), the focus was seen to be on that of the competent practitioner rather than the educated professional. If we examine some of the characteristics associated with professionalism, we can perhaps see the extent to which the model as shown here applies:

- Some autonomy for members of the profession. A true profession will be to some extent self-regulating and exercise influence over its members and not just be 'civil servants who are expected to toe the party line' (Beardall, 1995: 366, describing the possible future of teachers in South Africa).

- Responsibility and/or accountability. Hoyle (1995) argued that true professionalism is about responsibility, because it is more fundamental than accountability since there could be occasions when the responsibility could be in conflict with accountability to government. Bottery (1994) suggested that 'willing' accountability was the key.

- Being qualified and trained. Teaching is increasingly in many countries a graduate entry profession and tensions exist when personnel who are not qualified teachers teach in the classroom. In many developing countries, a shortage of qualified teachers makes this inevitable, but in several developed countries some argue that the 'craft' of teaching can be carried out by appropriately skilled practitioners, such as teaching assistants.

● Having a code of ethical practice. This is often best illustrated when breaches of a set of standards occur, and these can relate to duties which are expected as an almost basic requirement, such as punctuality and attendance, marking work and reporting to parents, to moral issues such as avoiding inappropriate relationships with students and, increasingly in this century, respecting resources.

The model of the professional learning teacher takes responsibility for his/ her own development, continually actively seeking appropriate 'training', but is accountable to colleagues, leaders, parents and above all students and pupils for improvement in the learning of this last group. He or she does not depend on others to regulate their development but through internal inquiry regularly seeks out improvement themselves, as well as seeking advice from colleagues and leaders. This teacher also respects a rigorous ethical code in carrying out internal investigation into personal and others' practices, ensuring that there is no harmful intrusion into colleagues' practices and that no student or pupil is in any way disadvantaged by the process. Overall, it may be seen as adding positively to developing notions of the teacher as an educated professional. This can only help in terms of the raised status of educationalists as they are perceived in all societies.

The third implication is that the role of students and pupils in developing their own learning, and thereby their role in school or college organization and management, will continue apace. This is a significant development in itself of course, but it can also be seen as part of a wider one, the continuing change in the relationship between learner and teacher. It is widely acknowledged that relationships lie at the core of effective teaching and learning, and thus the ability of both 'parties' to develop this relationship helped in part by some of the processes we have described here is fundamental.

A further interesting point is that, while our focus has been on practitioner research for all the reasons given, the processes and their impact lead practitioners to respect other research and expert researchers much more. Thus, the suspicious views of some teachers towards 'academic' research, mentioned by Richard Parker in Chapter Seven, are dissolved and the practitioners begin to value research as such. Now, instead of seeing it as remote and irrelevant to their daily work, they are able to apply a critical eye to research carried out by others, in universities for example, and more readily acknowledge its value and assess its relevance to themselves, as we suggest in Chapter Six. They are able to see that often the scale of such research, way beyond practitioners' possibilities, is important, partly because they can still recognize some of the basically similar techniques and processes that they have used. At one level, even reading academic reports as part of professional learning becomes more accessible, and hopefully, much more part of the norm in personal professional development. It could be argued that this is also a further way in which academic research is held to account for high standards, since the readership of research reports will be a critically aware one!

Another implication is that the role of leaders at all levels within an educational organization will become even more crucial, particularly in fostering a culture of professional learning within and across teams. This will apply to middle leaders as much as senior leaders, because it is they who deal with the daily work of staff where most of the crucial interaction occurs. This development of a middle leader's role relates both to within their own institution and across boundaries into others. As probably senior leaders spend more and more time out of their own individual schools or colleges, developing collaborative networks in various forms, so middle leaders become even more important in developing this culture in the 'home' base. This collective capacity within teams or institutions is well described by Fullan (2010: 72) when he reminds us that 'ordinary people – accomplish extraordinary things'.

The encouraging thing here is that from this development, stronger leadership at senior level is likely to emerge (Harrison, 2014) and this in itself will encourage even more effective leaders, so that, as Middlewood (2010) suggested, the criteria for effective leadership in the future could include its ability to generate more effective leaders for the future, forming an 'ever virtuous circle'. In that context, professional learning becomes self-perpetuating. That also can help greatly in the development of what is for many an ideal of a self-improving school system which Hargreaves (2012) describes as being a huge step towards maturity, and ultimately underpinning for him the collective moral purpose of such a system.

Which factors may affect future possibilities?

Although it has been argued (e.g. Middlewood et al., 2005) that the twenty-first century is the century of learning, as opposed to the twentieth century being one of teaching, there is still a tension between the two approaches to education and to teaching and learning across the world. On the one hand, there is undeniably a need for people to develop their creativity, independence in learning and ability to solve problems, it is also clear that the need for basic skills such as literacy and numeracy and in IT to be widespread remains. It is far too simplistic to suggest that this is a distinction between developed and developing countries, because the governments of several developed countries often still express concern about their young people's lack of basic skills. In an ideal world, a balance between mastery of these skills and the ability to be independent learners, take risks, would be flexible and creativity would exist. Countries such as Japan which achieve very high scores in measurable testing in basic subjects such as literacy, Maths and Science, also worry about their young people's lack of creativity and willingness to take risks, while some such as England who score highly in these areas worry about the relatively low ratings achieved in international comparison tables for those basic subjects. On the other hand, it is also clear that in those developing countries where universal education is still not available, the first need will be for ensuring basic skills for all children and the development needs of those teaching them will reflect this.

All this is relevant because the way in which serving teachers are developed or trained relates to the nature of the education which they are intended to provide. The form and nature of their professional learning therefore will be dictated primarily by the kind of learning which their own pupils, students or scholars are seen to require. With the growth of new technologies, and the global spread of education generally, a need for fostering basic skills will continue, as noted. Even in advanced societies, new skills emerge as needing to be learned (e.g. in mastering new forms of technological equipment) and where these are required, the training of those to teach them will continue to be needed; this can take the form of a relatively simple cascade model of what is basically instructional teaching. It is even possible that technology itself can provide the teaching in the future, as it does already in some areas, such as self-teaching computers. In such circumstances, one size DOES fit all and all can be trained similarly.

However, as the chapters of this book have shown, and as many others that we have referred to also show, teachers are first and foremost individual people and not robots or clones! Their personal development as people is also part and parcel of their professional development as teachers, hence our use of the term 'professional learning'. We believe that only through teachers developing their own individual creativity and independently establishing their own way of helping to instil a love of learning in their students will future adults and citizens develop effectively. By stressing individuality, we do not of course advocate anarchy(!); intelligent people note what works elsewhere and adopt or adapt it to their own thinking and practice. Consistency is the key, but not uniformity. Students however have a right to expect consistency in effective practice, and the best teachers adapt such practice to attune with what they have found works best for them individually. This is why we have argued for a consistent approach to identifying needs leading to the individual drawing on the findings to develop his or her own improved practice.

It is certain that changes will continue apace over the coming decades, and it is therefore all the more important that the search for underlying 'truths' continues, as to what enables teachers, students and indeed all people to learn effectively. Research or inquiry will play an absolutely crucial role in this and that is why a school or college culture based on in-house inquiry never rests but is continually striving to discover the best way forward.

Clearly, factors such as how consistency but not uniformity across groups or chains of schools is achieved, and the nature of external inspection regimes in terms of how these rate success will play a large part in all this. Probably, the most important factor will be how educational leaders of schools and colleges prioritize and manage such priorities in the future. Our contention would be that if these leaders have themselves been able to develop their own professional learning in the ways described in this book, then they will necessarily place the professional learning of the people for whom they are responsible as of the highest priority.

Summary of Chapter Eleven

This chapter has briefly:

- reflected on the significance of professional learning as exemplified in this book,

- drawn a few basic conclusions from the content,

- discussed some of the implications of these for future practices in education and

- suggested some of the factors which will impact on the extent to which these practices go forward.

REFERENCES

Abbott, I. and T. Bush (2013), 'Establishing and Maintaining High-Performing Leadership Teams: A Primary Perspective'. *Education 3–13*, Vol. 41, No. 6: 586–602.

Abbott, I., H. Constable and J. Norton (1991), *Case Studies in School Development Planning*. Sunderland: Sunderland Polytechnic.

Abbott, I., D. Middlewood and S. Robinson (2012), *Evaluation of the Primary School Improvement Group for Birmingham LA*. Warwick: University of Warwick.

Abbott, I., D. Middlewood and S. Robinson (2013), 'Prospecting for Support in a Wild Environment: Investigating a School-to-School Support System for Primary School Leaders'. *School Leadership & Management*, Vol. 34, No. 5: 439–53.

Abbott, I., M. Rathbone and P. Whitehead (2013), *Education Policy*. London: Sage.

Alsaeedi, F. and T. Male (2013), 'Transformational Leadership and Globalization: Attitudes of School Principals in Kuwait', *E M A L*, Vol. 41, No. 5: 640–57.

Altrichter, H., A. Feldman, P. Posch and B. Somekh (2008), *Teachers Investigate Their Work*. London: Routledge.

Angus, L. (2006), 'Educational Leadership and the Imperative of Including Student Voice, Student Interests and Students' Lives in the Mainstream'. *International Journal of Leadership in Education*, Vol. 9, No. 4: 369–79.

Antikanen, A. (2006), 'In Search of the Nordic Model in Education'. *Scandinavian Journal of Educational Policy*, Vol. 50, No. 3: 229–43.

Arendt, H. (1993), *Men in Dark Times*. San Diego, CA: Harcourt Brace.

Argyris, C. and DA Schon (1978), *Organizational Learning*. Cambridge, MA: Blackwell Publisher.

Argyris, C. and DA Schon (1995), *Organizational Learning II: Theory, Method and Practice*. Reading, MA: Addison-Wesley.

Arnold, R. (2006), 'Schools in Collaborations: Federations, Collegiate and Partnerships'. EMIE Report no. 86, National Foundation for Educational Research, Slough.

Arnot, M. and D. Reay (2007), 'A Sociology of Pedagogic Voice'. *Discourses*, Vol. 28: 327–42.

Ashraf, H. and J. Rarieya (2008), 'Teacher Development through Reflective Conversations'. *Reflective Practice: International Perspectives*, Vol. 9, No. 3: 269–79.

Aspinwall, K. and M. Pedlar (1997), 'Schools as Learning Organisations'. In B. Fidler, S. Russell and T. Simpkins (eds), *Choices for Self-Managing Schools*. London: Paul Chapman.

Attwood, T. and K. Bland (2012), 'Deployment and Impact of Higher Level Teaching Assistants: How Do Small-Scale Studies Fit into the Bigger Picture?'. *Management in Education*, Vol. 26, No. 2: 82–8.

Bauer, S. and D. Brazer (2012), 'Using Research to Lead School Improvement'. London: Sage.

Bell, L. and R. Bolam (2010), 'Teacher Professionalism and Continuing Professional Development: Contested Concepts and Their Implications for School Leaders'. In T. Bush, L. Bell and D. Middlewood (eds), *The Principles of Educational Leadership & Management*. London: Sage.

BERA (2014), *Research and the Teaching Profession: Building the Capacity for a Self-Improving System* London: BERA.

Best, R. (2000), 'The Training and Support Needs of Deputy Headteachers'. *Professional Development Today*, Vol. 4, No. 1: 39–50.

Bezzina, C. (2008), 'Towards a Learning Community: The Journey of a Maltese Catholic Church School'. *Management in Education*, Vol. 22, No. 3: 22–7.

Blandford, S. (2000), *Managing Professional Development in Schools*. London: Routledge.

Blasé, J. and J. Blasé (2004), 'Effective Instructional Leadership: How Principals Promote Teaching and Learning in School'. *Journal of Educational Administration*, Vol. 38, No. 2: 130–41.

Bolam, R., G. Dunning and P. Karstanje (eds) (2000), *New Heads in the New Europe*. Munster, NY: Waxmann.

Bradshaw, M. and P. Farrell (2002), *Teaching Assistants*. London: David Fulton.

Bragg, S. (2007), 'But I Listen to Children Anyway!-Teacher Perspectives on Pupil Voice'. *Educational Action Research*, Vol. 5, No. 4: 505–18.

Briggs, A. (2010), 'Monitoring and Evaluating Learning'. In T. Bush and L. Bell (eds), *Principles and Practice of Educational Management*. London: Sage.

Brighouse, T. (1991), *What Makes a Good School?* Stafford: Network Educational Press.

Brooks, V. (2012), 'Key Issues, Opportunities and Challenges for New Teachers'. In V. Brooks, I. Abbott and P. Huddleston (eds), *Preparing to Teach in Secondary Schools*. Maidenhead: Open University Press.

Bryk, A., P. Sebring, E. Allensworth, S. Luppescu and J. Easton (2010), *Organizing Schools for Improvement: Lessons from Chicago*. Chicago: University of Chicago Press.

Burn, K. and T. Mutton (2014), *Integrated ITE Programmes Based on 'Research-Informed Clinical Practice*. London: BERA.

Burnitt, M. and H. Gunter (2013), 'Primary School Councils: Organisation, Composition and Head Teacher Perceptions'. *Management in Education*, Vol. 27, No. 2: 56–62.

Bush, T. and D. Middlewood (2013), *Leading and Managing People in Education*. 3rd edition. London: Sage.

Cameron, D. and N. Clegg (2010), 'Foreword' by the Prime Minister and the Deputy Prime Minister. In *The Importance of Teaching: Schools White Paper*. London: Stationery Office.

Capstick, J. (2013), 'Practice Based Enquiry'. *The Teaching Leaders Quarterly*, Vol. 1, No. Q2/13: 14–15.

Carnell, E. (2001), 'The Value of Meta-Learning Dialogue'. *Professional Development Today*, Vol. 4, No. 2: 43–54.

Carnell, E. and C. Lodge (2002), *Supporting Effective Learning*. London: Paul Chapman Publications.

Connelly, M. and C. James (2006), 'Collaboration for School Improvement. a Resource Dependency and Institutional Framework for Analysis'. *Educational Management Administration and Leadership*, Vol. 34, No. 1: 69–87.

Cordingley, P., M. Bell and S. Thomason. (2004), 'Continuing Professional Development: The Evidence Base'. Centre for Use of Research and Evidence in Education, University of Manchester.

Craft, A. (1996), *Continuing Professional Development: A Practical Guide for Teachers and Schools*. London: Routledge and the Open University Press

D'Ambrosia, B. (1998), 'Using Research as a Stimulus for Learning'. *Journal for Research into Mathematics, Educational Monograph*, No. 9: 145–75.

Dalin, P. and V. Rust (1996), *Towards Schooling for the Twenty First Century*. London: Cassell.

Day, C. (1999), *Developing Teachers: The Challenges of Lifelong Learning*. London: Falmer Press.

Day, C. (2011), *The Routledge International Handbook of Teacher and School Development*. London: Routledge.

Department for Education (2010), *The Importance of Teaching: Schools White Paper*. London: Stationery Office.

DfE (2010), *The Importance of Teaching: Schools White Paper*. London: Stationery Office.

Durbin, B. and J. Nelson (2014), *Why Effective Use of Evidence in the Classroom Needs System-Wide Change*. Slough: NFER.

Early, P. and S. Bubb (2004), *Leading and Managing Continuing Professional Development*. London: Paul Chapman Publishing.

Elliot, J. (1984), 'Improving the Quality of Teaching through Action Research'. *Forum*, Vol. 26, No. 1: 44–58.

Emira, M. (2011), 'I Am More Than a TA!' *Management in Education*, Vol. 25, No. 4: 163–74.

Fielding, M., S. Bragg and J. Craig (2005), *Transfer of Good Practice*. Nottingham: DFES Publications.

Fielding, M. (2006), 'Leadership, Student Engagement, and the Necessity of Person-Centred Education'. *International Journal of Leadership in Education*, Vol. 9, No. 4: 299–313.

Flitton, L. and P. Warwick (2012), 'From Classroom Analysis to Whole School CPD: Promoting Talk as a Tool for Learning'. *British Educational Research Journal*, Vol. 29, No. 2: 99–121.

Flutter, J. and J. Ruddock (2004), *Consulting Pupils: What's in It for Schools?* London: Routledge.

Frost, R. (2008), 'Developing Student Participation, Research and Leadership'. *School Leadership and Management*, Vol. 28, No. 4: 353–68.

Fullan, M. (2001), *Leading in a Culture of Change*. San Francisco: Jossey-Bass.

Fullan, M. (2012), *All Systems Go: The Change Imperative for Whole System Reform*. Ontario: Corwin Press.

Galloway, S. (2000), 'Issues and Challenges in Continuing Professional Development: Looking Ahead'. Proceedings of a symposium by the Centre on Skills, Knowledge and Organisational Performance. Oxford, May.

Godfrey, D. (2014), 'Leadership of Schools as Research-Led Organisations in the English Educational Environment: Cultivating a Research-Engaged School Culture'. Educational Management Administration and Leadership. iFirst.

Goldacre, B. (2013), 'Building Evidence into Education' (online). Available at: http://media.education.gov.uk/assets/files/pdf/b/ben%20goldacre%20paper.pdf

Gordon, L. (1992), 'Educational Reform in New Zealand'. *International Studies in Sociology of Education*, No. 2: 23–42.

Groom, B. (2006), 'Building Relationships for Learning: The Developing Role of the TA'. *Support for Learning*, Vol. 21, No. 4: 199–203.

Gunter, H., D. Hall, and C. Mills (eds) (2014). *Education Policy Research: Design and Practice in a Time of Rapid Reform*. London: Bloomsbury.

Gunter, H. and P. Thomson (2007), 'But, Where Are the Children?'. Management in Education, Vol. 21, No. 1: 23–8.

Guskey, T. (1995), 'Professional Development in Education: In Search of the Optimal Mix'. In T. Guskey and M. Huberman (eds), *Professional Development in Education: New Paradigms and Practices*. New York: Teachers College Press.

Handscombe, G. and J. McBeath (2010), *The Research-Engaged School*. Chelmsford: Essex County Council.

Hargreaves, A. and Fink (2006), *Sustainable Leadership*. San Francisco: Jossey Bass.

Hargreaves, D. (1996), 'Teaching as Research-Based Profession: Possibilities and Prospects'. Paper presented at the Teacher Training Agency Annual Lecture, April. Available at: http://eppi.ioe.ac.uk/cms/Portals/0.PDF%20reviews%20 and%20summaries/TTA%20Hargreaves%20lecture.pdf

Hargreaves, D. (2010), *Creating a Self-Improving School System*. Nottingham: National College for School Leadership.

Hargreaves, D. (2012), *A Self-Improving School System: Towards Maturity*. Nottingham: National College for School Leadership.

Hargreaves, D. (2012a), *Leading a Self-Improving School System*. Nottingham: National College for School Leadership.

Hargreaves, D. and M. Fullan (2012), *Professional Capital. Transforming Teaching in Every School*. New York: Routledge.

Hargreaves, D. and D. Hopkins (1991), *The Empowered School*. London: Cassell.

Harris, A. (2002), *School Improvement: What's in It for Schools?* London: Routledge.

Harris, A. and M. Jones (2010), 'PLCs and System Improvement'. *Improving Schools*, Vol. 13, No. 2: 172–81.

Harris, H. (2008), *Distributed Leadership: Developing Tomorrow's Leaders*. London: Routledge.

Harrison, L. (2014), 'Mining from the Middle', *Teaching Leaders Quarterly*, 5th edition. London: Teaching Leaders.

Herr, K. and G. Anderson (2008), 'Teacher Research and Learning Communities: A Failure to Theorize Power Relations?', *Language Arts*, Vol. 85, No. 5: 382–91.

Heystek, J. (2007), 'Reflecting on Principals as Managers or Moulded Leaders in a Managerialist School System'. *South African Journal of Education*, Vol. 27, No. 3: 491–505.

Hillage, J., R. Pearson and A. Anderson. (1998), *Excellence in Research on Schools: Research Report RR74*. London: Department of Education and Employment.

Hoffer, E. (1963), *The Ordeal of Change*. London: Penguin Books.

Holyoke, L., P. Sturko, N. Wood and L. Wu (2012), 'Are Academic Departments Perceived as Learning Organisations?' *Educational Management Administration and Leadership*, Vol. 40, No. 4: 436–48.

Honingh, M. and E. Hooge (2014), 'The Effect of Leader Support on Teacher Collaboration in Dutch Primary and Secondary Schools'. *Educational Management Administration and Leadership*, Vol. 42, No. 1: 75–98.

Hoyle, E. (1995), 'Changing Conceptions of a Profession'. In H. Busher and L. Saran (eds), *Managing Teachers as Professionals in Schools*. London: Kogan Page.

Huillet, D., J. Adler and M. Berger (2011), 'Teachers as Researchers: Placing Mathematics at the Core'. *Education as Change*, Vol. 15, No. 1: 17–32.

James, D. (2104), 'Taking the Guesswork Out of Education'. *TES professional*. 5 September 2014, 34–7.

Johnson, D. (1994), *Research Methods in Educational Management*. Harlow: Longman.

Judkins, M., O. Stacey, T. McCrone and M. Inniss (2014), *Teacher's Use of Research Evidence: A Case Study of United Learning Schools*. Slough: NFER.

Kanter, R. (1988), 'Change-Master Skills'. In R. Kuhn (ed.), *Handbook for Creative and Innovative Managers*. New York: McGraw-Hill.

Karstanje, P. (2000), 'New Heads in Five Countries'. In R. Bolam, G. Dunning and P. Karstanje (eds), *New Heads in the New Europe*. Munster, NY: Waxmann.

Kasl, E., V. Marsick and K. Declat (1997), 'Teams as Learners'. *The Journal of Behavioural Science*, Vol. 33: 227–46.

Katzenmeyer, M. and G. Moller (2001), *Awaking the Sleeping Giant*. Thousand Oaks: Corwin Press.

Kellett, M. (2005), *How to Develop Children as Researchers*. London: Paul Chapman Publishing.

Kent, P. (2012), 'The Case for Using Student Voice in Teacher Selection and Recruitment: Reflections from a School Leader'. *Management in Education*, Vol. 26, No. 3: 148–9.

King, F. (2011), 'The Role of Leadership in Developing and Sustaining Teachers' Professional Learning'. *Management in Education*, Vol. 25, No. 4: 149–55.

Knight, J., B. Lingford and L. Bartlett (1994), 'Reforming Teacher Education in Australia, 1989–1993'. *British Journal of Sociology of Education*, Vol. 15: 451–66.

Koshy, V. (2008), *Action Research for Improving Educational Practice*. London: Sage.

Kydd, L. (2012), 'Relational Agency and Pre-Service Trainee Teachers: Using Student Voice to Frame Teacher Education Pedagogy'. *Management in Education*, Vol. 25, No. 4: 149–55.

Lambert, L. G. (2007), 'Lasting Leadership: Towards Sustainable School Improvement'. *Journal of Educational Change*, Vol. 8, No. 4: 311–22.

Law, S. and D. Glover (2000), *Educational Leadership and Learning*. Buckingham: Open University Press.

Leithwood, K., C. Day, P. Sammons, A. Harris and D. Hopkins (2010 re-issued), Seven Strong Claims about Successful School Leadership. London: DfES.

Levin, B., A. Cooper, S. Arjomand, K. Thompson (2011), 'Can Simple Interventions Increase Research Use in Secondary Schools?' *Canadian Journal of Educational Administration Policy*, Vol. 126: 1–29.

Liebermann, A. and Friedrich (2007), 'Changing Teachers from within: Teachers as Leaders'. In J. MacBeath and Y. C. Cheng (eds), *Leadership for Learning: International Perspectives*. Amsterdam: Sense.

Lightbody, T. (2012), *Outstanding Teaching and Learning*. 2nd edition. London: Collegenet.

Liljenberg, M. (2014), 'Distributing Leadership to Establish Developing and Learning School Organisations in the Swedish Context'. *Educational Management, Administration and Leadership*. Vol. 43, No. 1: 152–70.

Lilly, J., A. Peacock, S. Shoveller and D. Struthers (2014), *Beyond Levels: Alternative Assessment Approaches*. Nottingham: National College for Teaching and Leadership.

Lindsay, H. (2015), *Adaptability :The Secret to Lifelong Learning for Professionals*. London: ICEAW/PARN.

Lockhorst, D., A. Wilfried and A. Pilot (2010), 'CSCL in Teacher Training: What Learning Tasks Lead to Collaboration?'. *Technology, Pedagogy and Education*, Vol. 19, No. 1: 63–78.

Lowstead, J., P. Larsson, and S. Karsten (2007), *From Intensified Work to Professional Development. A Journey through European School*. Brussels: Peter Lang.

Lumby, J. (2001), 'Framing the Curriculum for the Twenty First Century'. In D. Middlewood and N. Burton (eds), *Managing the Curriculum*. London: Paul Chapman Publishing.

Mattar, D. (2012), 'Instructional Leadership in Lebanese Public Schools'. *Educational Management Administration and Leadership*, Vol. 40, No. 4: 509–31.

McCharen, B., J. Song and J. Martens (2011), 'School Innovation: The Mutual Impacts of Organisational Learning and Creativity'. *Educational Management Administration and Leadership,* Vol. 39, No. 6: 676–94.

McGregor, J. (2004), *Students as Researchers*. Cranfield: National College for School Leadership.

McGuigan, P. (2008), *Professional Development through Enquiry Based Practice*. Leeds: CapeUK.

Menter, I., D. Elliott, J. Hall, S. Hall, M. Hulme, J. Lewin and K. Lowden (2010), A *Guide to Practitioner Research in Education*. London: Sage.

Middlewood, D. (1997), 'Managing Staff Development'. In T. Bush and D. Middlewood (eds), *Managing People in Education*. London: Paul Chapman Publishing.

Middlewood, D. (2001), 'The Future of Managing Teacher Performance and Appraisal'. In D. Middlewood and C. Cardno (eds), *Managing Teacher Performance and Appraisal: A Comparative Approach*. London: Routledge.

Middlewood, D. (2010), 'Managing People and Performance'. In T. Bush, L. Bell and D. Middlewood (eds), *Principles of Educational Leadership and Management*. London: Sage.

Middlewood, D. and I. Abbott (2012), *Achieving Success in Your Leadership Project*. London: Sage.

Middlewood, D., M. Coleman and J. Lumby (1998), *Practitioner Research in Education: Making a Difference*. London: Paul Chapman Publishing.

Middlewood, D., M. Coleman and J. Lumby (1999), *Practitioner Research in Education*. London: Paul Chapman.

Middlewood, D. and R. Parker (2009), *Leading and Managing Extended Schools*. London: Sage.

Middlewood, D., R. Parker and J. Beere (2005), *Creating a Learning School*. London: Paul Chapman Publishing.

Middlewood, D., R. Parker and J. Piper-Gale (2011), *Learning through Research*. Leicester: Flexpress.

Mitra, D. (2009), 'Collaborating with Students: Building Youth-Adult Partnerships in Schools'. *American Journal of Education*, Vol. 115: 407–36.

Morris, A. and J. Hiebert (2011), 'Creating Shared Instructional Products'. *Educational Researcher*, Vol. 40, No. 1: 5–15.

Mortimore, P. (2013), *Education Under Siege*. London: Policy Press.

Muijs, D. and A. Harris (2006), 'Teacher Led School Improvement: Teacher Leadership in the UK'. *Teaching and Teacher Education*, Vol. 22, No. 8: 961–72.

Naylor, D. (1999), 'The Professional Development Needs of Mid-Day Assistants'. *Professional Development Today*, Vol. 3, No. 1: 51–60.

NCTL (2014), *Impact of Teaching Schools*. London: NCTL.

Nehring, J. and G. Fitzsimons (2011), 'The PLC as Subversive Activity'. *Professional Development in Education*, Vol. 37, No. 4: 513–35.

Nelson, J. and O'Beirne (2014), *Using Evidence in the Classroom: What Works and Why?* Slough: NFER.

O'Sullivan (1997), 'Learning Organisations Reengineering Schools for Lifelong Learning'. *School Leadership and Management: Formerly School Organisation*, Vol. 17, No. 2: 217–30.

OECD (2013), 'Education Policy Outlook-Finland'. Available at: http:www.oecd. org/edu/EDUCATION.

Ofsted (2009), *Inspection Report on Forest Primary School*. London: Ofsted.

Ozga, J. (1995), 'Deskilling a Profession'. In H. Busher and L. Saran (eds), *Managing Teachers as Professionals in Schools*. London: Kogan Page.

Parker, R. (2011), 'The Impact on School Culture'. In D. Middlewood, R. Parker and J. Piper-Gale (eds), *Learning through Research*. Leicester: Flexpress.

Piggot-Irvine, E. (2010), 'One School's Approach to Overcoming Resistance and Improving Appraisal: Organizational Learning in Action'. *Educational Management Administration and Leadership*, Vol. 38, No. 2: 229–45.

Pont, B. (2008), 'Improving School Leadership'. *Policy and Practice*. Paris: OECD Publishing, 1.

Revans, R. (1982), *The Origins and Growth of Action Learning*. Bromley: Chartwell-Bratt.

Rhodes, C. and M. Brundrett (2010), 'Leadership for Learning'. In T. Bush, L. Bell and D. Middlewood (eds), *Principles of Educational Leadership and Management*. London: Sage.

Ribbins, P. (2008), 'A Life and Career-Based Framework for the Study of Leaders in Education'. In J. Lumby, G. Crow and P. Pashiardis (eds), *International*

Handbook on the Preparation and Development of School Leaders. London: Routledge.

Robinson, S. (2012), 'Five Signs of Effective CPD'. *LDR Magazine*. Nottingham: National College for School Leadership.

Robinson, V. (2007), *School Leadership and Student Outcomes: Identifying What Works and Why*. Melbourne: Australian Council of Leaders.

Russell, T. (2005), 'Can Reflective Practice Be Taught?'. *Reflective Practice*, Vol. 6, No. 2: 199–204.

Rutherford, D. and L. Jackson (2008), 'Collegiates as a Model for Collaboration'. *Management in Education*, Vol. 22, No. 3: 28–34.

Sahlberg, P. (2011), *Finnish Lessons: What Can Be Learned from Education in Finland?* New York: Teachers College Press.

Salokangas, M. and C. Chapman (2014), 'Exploring Governance in Two Chains of Academy Schools: A Comparative Case Study'. *Educational Management Administration and Leadership*, Vol. 42, No. 3: 372–86.

Sebba, J., P. Kent and J. Treganza (2012), *Powerful Professional Learning*. Nottingham: NCSL.

Senge, P. (1990), *The Fifth Discipline: The Art and Practice of the Learning Organisation*. London: Random House.

Sharp, C., A. Eames, D. Sanders and K. Tomlinson (2006), *Leading a Research-Engaged School*. Nottingham: National College for School Leadership.

Sharples, J. (2013), *Evidence for the Frontline*. London: Alliance for Useful Evidence. Available at: http://www.alliance4usefulevidence.org/assets/EVIDENCE-FOR-THE-FRONTLINE-FINAL-5-June-2013.pdf.

Simeon, J. (2009), 'Teacher Motivation in The Seychelles'. MA dissertation, University of Warwick (Unpublished).

Slater, L. (2004), 'Collaboration: A Framework for School Improvement'. *International Electronic Journal for Leadership*, Vol. 8, No. 5: 113–28.

Slater, L. (2008), 'Pathways to Building Leadership Capacity'. *Educational Management Administration and Leadership*, Vol. 36, No. 1: 55–69.

Smith, K. and K. Steiner Engelson (2012), 'Developing an Assessment for Learning Culture in School'. *International Journal of Leadership in Education: Theory and Practice*, Vol. 16, No. 1: 106–25.

Smith, P. and I. Abbott (2014), 'Local Responses to National Policy: The Contrasting Experiences of Two Midlands Cities to the Academies Act 2010'. *Educational Management Administration and Leadership*, Vol. 42, No. 3: 341–55.

Smyth, J. (2006), 'Educational Leadership That Fosters Student Voice'. *International Journal of leadership in Education*, Vol. 9, No. 4: 279–84.

Stevenson, H. (2007), 'Improvement through Collaboration and Competition: Can the Government Have It Both Ways?' *Management in Education*, Vol. 21, No. 4: 29–33.

Stoll, L., D. Fink and L. Earl (2003), *It's About Learning (and It's about Time)*. London: RoutledgeFalmer.

Stoll, L., R. Bolam and A. McMahon (2006), 'Professional Learning Communities: A Review of the Literature'. *Journal of Educational Change*, Vol. 7, No. 4: 221–58.

Tatto, M. T. (2014), *International Overview: The Contribution of Research to High-Performing Systems*. London: BERA.

Taysum, A. (2010), *Evidence Informed Leadership in Education*. London: Continuum.

Thomson, P. (2009), 'Consulting Secondary School Pupils about Their Learning'. *Oxford Review of Education*, Vol. 35, No. 6: 671–87.

Thomson, P. and H. Gunter (2007), 'From Consulting Pupils to Pupils as Researchers: A Situated Case Narrative'. *British Educational Research Journal*, Vol. 32, No. 6: 839–56.

Thorne, C. (2011), 'The Impact of Educational Reforms on the Work of the School Principal in the UAE'. *Educational Management Administration and Leadership*, Vol. 39, No. 2: 172–85.

Timperley, H. (2011), *Realising the Power of Professional Learning*. Buckingham: Open University Press.

Tooley, J. and D. Darby (1998), *Educational Research a Critique: A Survey of Published Educational Research*. London: Ofsted.

Townsend, A. (2010), 'Action Research'. In D. Hartas (ed.), *Educational Research and Inquiry*. London: Continuum.

Townsend, A. (2013), *Action Research: The Challenges of Understanding and Changing Practice*. Maidenhead: McGraw Hill.

United Nations (1997), *Portraits in Courage*. Paris: UN.

Watkins, C. (2001), 'Learning about Learning Enhances Performance'. *Research Matters*, No. 13, University of London' Contemporary.

Wenger, E. (1998), *Communities of Practice: Learning, Meaning and Identity*. New York: Cambridge University Press.

West-Burnham, J. (1994), 'Inspection, Evaluation and Quality Assurance'. In T. Bush and J. West-Burnham (eds), *Principles and Practice of Educational Management*. London: Sage.

West-Burnham, J. (2013), 'Contemporary Issues in Educational Leadership'. In M. Brundrett (ed.), *Principles of School Leadership*. London: Sage.

Whitty, G. and Wisby (2007), 'Whose Voice? An Exploration of the Current Policy Interest in Pupil Involvement in School Decision-Making'. *International Studies in Sociology of Education*, Vol. 17, No. 3: 303–19.

Widodo, A. and C. Riandi (2013), 'Dual Mode Professional Development: Challenges and Re-Visioning Future TPD in Indonesia'. *Teacher Development*, Vol. 17, No. 3: 380–92.

Woollard, J. (2012), 'When Teaching a Class of Daemons, Dragons, and Trainee Teachers-the Pedagogy of the Virtual Classroom'. *Management in Education*, Vol. 26, No. 2: 45–51.

Yin, H., J. Lee and W. Wang (2014), 'Dilemmas of Leading National Curriculum Reform in a Global Era: A Chinese Perspective'. *Educational Management Administration and Leadership*, Vol. 42, No. 2: 293–311.

Zhang, W. and M. Brundrett (2011), 'School Leaders' Perspectives on Leadership Learning: The Case for Informal and Experiential Learning'. *Management in Education*, Vol. 24, No. 4: 154–8.

SUBJECT INDEX